Praise for The Big Fun Guide t

Even after living in the area for decades I still found things in this bool l- aged children and I found activities that will still entertain us for years to c nt of the car so if we're out and about and need to kill time it'll be at my fi

You'll want to give a copy to the new neighbors when they move to town.

— *Carolyn Watterson*

This guide is quick and easy to use. Thanks for putting it together in such user-friendly format!

— *Laura Lauffer, PBO mom to Rhys and Riana*

One of my all time favorite sayings is, "The hardest thing to see is right under your nose." As a resident of this oh-so-unique area for two decades, I was blown away by how many wonderful things there are to do in this part of the country "right under my nose!"

Erin Donoghue Baldwin's book is a visual, informational, delectable delight of the view of our very own backyard and creates a great guide to the best this area has to offer the big, the little, and the in between of us.

As a preschool teacher, a mom, and a grandmom, I can only think of three words, "FIELDTRIP, FIELDTRIP, FIELDTRIP!"

— *Ms. Kathy, preschool teacher extraordinaire*

This book highlights many exciting things going on in our own backyard. As a mom, I'm always looking for something new to do with the kids. The Big Fun Guide provides information on all kinds of adventures within a few miles from home. A great book for families moving to the area and people already settled in!

— *Krista Millard, Chatham county mom*

I've lived in this area for 18 years, and the majority of these activities have never even crossed my radar!! What a great book for families new to the area, and to those of us who need to get out and discover our own backyards!

— *Julie Cummins*

I definitely enjoyed the book. As a relative newcomer to the Chapel Hill area (been here 3 years), Erin's book gave me a whole new list of things to do. As I was reading it, I was making notes in my planner about all the places I want to take the kids in the next few weeks! A few things really stood out to me:

- the organization of the sections made sense

- age appropriate comments are really helpful. As a mom to two kids under 5, not every "kid-friendly" activity is great for the younger ones

-On that same note, the park descriptions were really helpful, especially with children of different ages. At this point, it's important to have a fenced park (for the lightening fast 19 month old), but also a park that will not bore the 4.5 year old!

-Range of activities are great. I could open Erin's book when I'm feeling recharged on a Monday morning and find a great museum or historical adventure. Or, I could open Erin's book on a Thursday afternoon when naps seem to end way too early and we just need to get out of the house and run around at a park for a few hours. I can dazzle visitors with my knowledge of local festivals...Never will our playgroup spend days debating about what to do next week - Erin's book gave me plenty of ideas.

- It's refreshing to see a book about the Chapel Hill area that's meant for people that live here, and are looking for activities for children on a day to day basis instead of for a quick weekend visit.

-What a great idea to have descriptions in the library sections about what type of books they have at the libraries (age appropriate)!

- Great activities for all times of the year. I particularly liked having all the festivals listed in one place - you could just put them all on your calendar at the same time.

- Erin's humor and detailed descriptions make you feel like your having a conversation with your good friend about what to do with the kids. You can trust her because she includes the random points of interest that only a parent would. Does that playground have mulch that my 1 year old will eat? Are there any parks around here that have a fence so I don't spend the entire 2 hours at the playground chasing my 2 year old around? Where can I take my budding artist, history lover, or naturalist?

— *Jennifer Meffe*

The Big Fun Guide to Tar Heel Country:

135+ Activities for Families in Chapel Hill, Carrboro, Hillsborough, Pittsboro, and points in between!

By Erin Donoghue Baldwin

The Big Fun Guide to Tar Heel Country : 135 + Activities for Families in Chapel Hill, Carrboro, Hillsborough, Pittsboro, and Points in Between!

Attention schools, non-profits, and corporations: quantity discounts available for fundraisers and gifts. Please contact us!

Published by:
DRT Press
PO Box 427
Pittsboro, NC 27312
Tel: (919)360-7073 Fax: (866) 562-5040
www.drtpress.com

Printed in the United States of America on 30% post-consumer content paper.
Book design: Jeffrey W. Duckworth, www.duckofalltrades.com

Publisher's Cataloging-in-Publication data

Baldwin, Erin Donoghue.
The big fun guide to Tar Heel country : 135-plus activities for families in Chapel Hill, Carrboro, Hillsborough, Pittsboro, and points in between! / by Erin Donoghue Baldwin.
p. cm.
Includes index.
Contents: Museums and History -- Arts, Crafts & Music -- Parks and Playgrounds -- Hikes, Nature & Animals -- Recreation and Sports -- Swimming -- Boating--Gyms--Road Trips.
ISBN 1-933084-10-3
1. Chapel Hill (N.C.) -- Guidebooks. 2. Carrboro (N.C.) -- Guidebooks. 3. Pittsboro (N.C.)--Guidebooks. 4. Hillsborough (N.C.)--Guidebooks. 5. Orange County (N.C.)--Guidebooks. 6. Chatham County (N.C.)--Guidebooks. I. The big fun guide to Tar Heel Country : one hundred and thirty five-plus activities for families in Chapel Hill, Carrboro, Hillsborough, Pittsboro, and points in between! II. Title.

F264.C38 B35 2008
975.6/56 20--dc22 2008931274

10 9 8 7 6 5 4 3 2

Although the author has researched all sources to ensure accuracy, DRT Press can assume no responsibility for errors herein. Venue times, websites, phone numbers, and costs can change. Please call the attraction before visiting for the most current information. And above all, have BIG FUN!

NOTE FROM THE AUTHOR

It's easy to find guides for big metropolitan areas, and these publications generally do a good job describing well-known attractions such as big, flashy museums, shopping malls, and important historical sites. But what if you're headed to a smaller locale-- and nearly everyone ends up in one, to visit relatives or to take a new job-- where attractions are not so obvious? You'd like to ask someone about good places to let the kids run around, or an interesting place to spend a rainy Sunday afternoon, but where to turn? Hence, the origin of this book.

The Chapel Hill area isn't just about basketball, indie music, and the college set. From Hillsborough to the north and Pittsboro to the south, from Durham to the east and Burlington to the west, this area has an abundance of natural, historical, and cultural resources for individuals and families to enjoy. This is a region of communities deeply rooted in their history and traditions, combined with the diverse contributions of newcomers from across the state, nation, and world who are attracted by the area's prominence in education and research.

But all that can get too rarified without some down-to-earth observation. In these pages you'll find reviews of places and events, with such information as their suitability for younger or older children, for strollers or picnics. I've tried to go beyond the obvious, and strived to supplement basic information with knowledge that I've gained firsthand. And, because there are times that call for greater adventure, this guide includes day trips to special places such as the North Carolina Zoo in Asheboro and the children's museums in Raleigh and Greensboro.

As for the practical information: prices, hours, and dates listed here are as accurate as possible, but of course are subject to change. When in doubt, call ahead or, if possible, check the website—contact information is provided for nearly every entry. Most importantly, for any activity, consider foremost what your child or children can handle. While appropriate ages are listed for various places and activities, children naturally vary in their skills, interests, and temperaments.

I am indebted to many kind people for their help, but I must give special thanks to Anne Wander, Cherie Page, Peter Liao, Adrienne Bashista, and Ashley Nissler for their suggestions, knowledge, and insights. I'm lucky to know such talented people who use words well and love exploring this area and sharing their discoveries with others. For even though I grew up in Chapel Hill, I have found that there's a lot more to do here than I ever knew, and more is on its way. At the time of this writing, over a half dozen parks are scheduled for construction or renovation. Museums and libraries plan to expand, or move into larger quarters. New festivals are gaining traction and growing in popularity.

This is an exciting time to live in Tar Heel Country, and I hope you find in this guide activities and events providing worthwhile fun and good memories. Any time spent with a child is time well spent.

Erin Donoghue Baldwin

FOREWORD

Families are so busy these days. Parents are working. Kids are off to schools and childcare. Friday arrives and everyone's pooped! Then it's Saturday morning and you think, "What should we do this weekend?"

It's hard for parents to find the time to plan playful weekend activities together. What local parents need is a concise 'things-to-do' reference to all the local fun, family activities.

Well, look no further, weary Tar Heels! The Big Fun Guide to Tar Heel Country by Erin Donoghue Baldwin has a wonderful list of local family activities. Old favorites and new ideas are offered with helpful symbols to ease trip planning.

I've lived in Tar Heel Country for almost 20 years and have spent much time with my family enjoying local activities, but The Big Fun Guide has activities even I have not tried yet! I can't wait to check them out with my family.

We are so fortunate to live in one of the most beautiful, diverse, and accessible areas of the country. It's no wonder the Triangle has been rated the #1 place to live for so many years.

Erin has put together a list of the best activities in our area. Tired parents can quickly pick an activity for the family and be there in an hour or less!

See you in Tar Heel Country,

Evette Horton

Founder, Chapel Hill-Carrboro Mothers Club

GUIDE TO SYMBOLS

 Bathrooms

 Stroller-friendly

 Food nearby

 Picnic-friendly

Table of Contents

PART 1: MOSTLY INDOORS

MUSEUMS AND HISTORY

Ackland Art Museum

The Ackland Art Museum has a large collection of art and plenty of temporary exhibits, but what makes it a good outing for children is that it is small, and the diversity of works—European paintings, African masks, Mediterranean sculpture, Asian statuary, and arresting modern pieces—keeps children's attention.

The Education Resource Center, to the right of the entrance, has manipulatives, activities, books, and questions to prompt children to think about art in a new way: "What do you think the artist wanted you to know?" and "How are these two pieces of art the same? How are they different?" Objects such as sandpaper, tea balls filled with cloves or other scents, a white board with magnets and markers, and intriguing toys help children explore art's many possibilities. Some materials, such as notebooks and cards, are meant to go out into the galleries, so children can approach art with something tangible to help them understand what they see. Everything is labeled for a specific age group, which makes choosing appropriate materials easy.

The museum hosts a variety of events to connect the community with art, from yoga and art classes to literary and music events. Call the museum or check the website for details. Even on a regular day, visiting the Ackland can be an adventure. Be sure to notice the birds on the roof when you leave!

Hours: Wednesday through Saturday 10am - 5pm, Sunday 1pm - 5pm. Open until 9pm on the 2nd Friday of every month. Closed New Year's Day, July 4th, Thanksgiving Day, Christmas Eve, and Christmas Day. Closed Monday and Tuesday.

Contact Info:
Phone: (919) 966-5736
Website: www.ackland.org/index.php
Street address: 101 South Columbia Street, Chapel Hill

Bathrooms: yes
Stroller-friendly: yes
Food nearby: yes
Picnic-friendly: not specifically, but there are lots of places outside and on campus
Recommended ages: any, but especially preschool and up

Cost: free

Burwell School Historic Site

The Burwell School is a carefully restored house in historic Hillsborough. Originally a school for girls, it later became a residence through the Civil War. Free, docent-led tours, based on letters and journals from Mrs. Burwell, slave Elizabeth Hobbes Keckly, and former students, follow the history of the house up until the Civil War. The self-guided "Beehive Tour" details the history of the home when the Collins family inhabited the premises during the Civil War era. Several books about the house are available for purchase inside, including the novel *On Agate Hill,* by renowned author and Hillsborough resident Lee Smith.

Behind the main house, the Music Room holds one of the original classrooms, and the restored brick necessary stands at the edge of the garden. The self-guided tour of the Carrie Waitt Spurgeon Garden describes the restoration in 2004 using historical documents from the Burwells' son, the detailed journals of Anna Burwell herself, and local reports over time as the Spurgeon family resided there the following seventy years.

The Burwell School hosts events throughout the year, such as concerts and lectures, and is available for private events as well.

Hours: February through December, Wednesday through Saturday 11am – 4pm, Sunday 1pm – 4pm, and by appointment

Contact Info:
Phone: (919) 732-7451
Website: www.burwellschool.org
Street Address: 319 North Churton Street, Hillsborough

Bathrooms: yes
Stroller-friendly: no
Food nearby: yes
Picnic-friendly: yes
Recommended ages: all, though 6 and up may enjoy it more

Cost: free

Carolina Basketball Museum

On the first floor of the new Ernie Williamson Athletics Center, this new 8,000-square-foot museum of UNC basketball features a theater, displays, and a 32-foot tower for visitors to "make their own calls" on great Carolina plays. One room is dedicated solely to UNC victories. The museum has artifacts and videos about the history of UNC basketball, including memorabilia, such as uniforms and trophies, and the contributions of Dean Smith. Interactive displays recreate historic games and list biographical and statistical information on every UNC player, past and present. A must for Tar Heel fans or initiates. Parking is available across the street in the Smith lot.

Hours: Monday through Friday 9am - 4pm. Weekday game days, 10am until one hour before game. Weekend game days, open three and half hours before game until one hour before game.

Contact Info:
Phone: (919) 843-2000
Website: www.carolinabasketballmuseum.com
Street address: 450 Skipper Bowles Drive, Chapel Hill

Bathrooms: yes
Stroller-friendly: yes
Food nearby: no
Picnic-friendly: no
Recommended ages: any

Cost: free

Carrboro Branch Library

Because of its partnership with the McDougle Schools' Media Center, the Carrboro Branch Library offers the town's best selection of books for beginning readers. While patrons may borrow only a limited number of McDougle school books, the variety of series, easy readers, and chapter books provides plenty of practice with new material. Moreover, because fewer people visit this library, chances are better you'll find any popular books, for adults or children, that may be checked out elsewhere. Be aware, however: the Carrboro Library is a branch of the Orange County system. Books should not be returned to the Chapel Hill Public Library.

Carrboro Branch Library also offers many of the same children's programs as Chapel Hill Public Library, including weekly story times for toddlers and preschoolers.

The limited operating hours make dropping in at the Carrboro Branch Library more difficult, but once there, be sure to peruse the children and family videos and audio books, as well as the adult titles against the back wall.

Hours: Monday through Thursday 3:30pm - 8pm, Saturday 10am - 2pm, Sunday 1pm - 5pm. Closed Friday.

Contact Info:
Phone: (919) 969-3006
Website: co.orange.nc.us/library/carrboro/index.htm
Street address: McDougle Middle School Media Center, 900 Old Fayetteville Road, Chapel Hill

Bathrooms: yes
Stroller-friendly: yes
Food nearby: no
Picnic-friendly: yes (outside)
Recommended ages: any

Cost: free

Chapel Hill Museum

This building, once the Chapel Hill Public Library, now houses the Chapel Hill Preservation Society and its museum dedicated to the town's history. Permanent exhibits on singer James Taylor and Franklin Street find appeal with older children, while the antique fire engine is a hit with younger kids. The collection of North Carolina pottery has examples of some of area's the best known potters. Annually the museum holds a public art project, such as the self-portrait exhibit, to which community members contribute works. At the end, everyone gathers for the presentation and has fun seeing what folks came up with.

Though there is not a lot here for little ones, it is a quick, quiet place with a nice gift shop. Afterwards, enjoy a picnic on the grassy lawn of the Horace Williams House, which is a short walk east down Franklin Street, or head downtown for rest and refreshment.

Hours: Wednesday through Saturday 10am - 4pm, Sunday 1pm - 4pm. Closed Monday and Tuesday.

Contact Info:
Phone: (919) 967-1400
Website: www.chapelhillmuseum.org
Street address: 523 East Franklin Street, Chapel Hill

Bathrooms: yes
Stroller-friendly: yes
Food nearby: no
Picnic-friendly: no
Recommended ages: any, but 6 and up may enjoy it more

Cost: free; donations accepted

Chapel Hill Public Library

The Chapel Hill Public Library houses a wide selection of books, audio books, and CDs. New books for young adult and adult titles are easy to find near the entrance of the main library. New children's books are just inside the children's section. Because this library is very active and serves a large reading public, finding popular books can be challenging, especially during the school year. While the book you want may be checked out, you can place a hold on it for free.

The library has many programs and events for children—time for toddlers, story time for preschoolers, and book clubs for older children, as well as movies and performances. The children's section has magazines, computers, and plenty of tables and chairs for curling up to read. Librarians regularly rotate featured books by season or holiday, and will gladly help or answer questions. The restroom in this section, incidentally, is usually cleaner and more family-friendly than the larger, gender-only restrooms in the lobby.

On your way out, be sure to notice the fliers, newspapers, and publications, including the Parks and Recreation catalogs and bus schedules, free for the taking. Take a minute to view the changing exhibit of local art displayed throughout the stairwell and downstairs.

Hours: Monday through Thursday 10am - 9pm, Friday 10am - 6pm, Saturday 9am - 6pm, Sunday 1pm - 8pm. Closed holidays.

Contact Info:
Phone: (919) 968-2777
Website: www.chapelhillpubliclibrary.org
Street address: 100 Library Drive, Chapel Hill

Bathrooms: yes
Stroller-friendly: yes
Food nearby: yes
Picnic-friendly: no
Recommended ages: any

Cost: free

Felicity Day

Named for the American Girl doll, this event is a day of historic fun for both girls and boys. Most children dress up in long dresses, mob caps, or three-cornered hats, and just watching them walk down the street is charming. You'll want to bring your camera.

The activities run concurrently, and separate activities are scheduled for boys and girls. Groups rotate between events, so no place is too crowded. Some children learn a rather intricate Colonial dance, while others participate in a musket drill. At the Burwell School, children learn about colonial times and make friends while having lemonade in the dining room. In another building, children make a period craft. The staff members leading the activities are good with children and very knowledgeable. The tickets list the schedule and location, so knowing what to do and when is relatively clear. While the children are busy, adults may tour the historic site or hear about the site's history. There's even a costume contest, and children may be photographed at the museum. The photographs are later available for purchase online. It's a good idea to register in advance—tickets are available at the Orange County Historical Museum.

Hours: first Saturday in September, 10am - 4pm

Contact Info:
Phone: (877) 732-7748 or (919) 732-7741
Website: www.historichillsborough.org
Street address: 150 East King Street, Hillsborough

Bathrooms: yes
Stroller-friendly: yes
Food nearby: yes
Picnic-friendly: not in the buildings, but there are some places nearby
Recommended ages: 6-13

Cost: $6

Historic Hillsborough Thematic Children's Tours

The Alliance for Historic Hillsborough uses the unique sites and buildings of Hillsborough to teach children about history, architecture, and government. For early elementary students, grades K-3, tours focus on town government. Older children, grades 5-8, can learn about the architectural history of Hillsborough from Native American settlements to the nineteenth century. A tour of old schools teaches children in grades 3-6 about what education used to be like. Most tours last about an hour and include role-playing and hands-on activities. They are open to any group of ten children or more, with one adult per ten children required. Make reservations at least two weeks in advance.

Hours: by appointment

Contact Info:
Phone: (919) 732-7741 or (877) 732-7748
Website: www.historichillsborough.org
Street address: Alexander Dickson House, 150 East King Street, Hillsborough

Bathrooms: yes
Stroller-friendly: yes
Food nearby: yes
Picnic-friendly: not on tour, but there are many spots nearby
Recommended ages: K-8th grade

Cost: $2 per child, adults free

Kidzu Children's Museum

Kidzu has interactive, educational exhibits for children that change a couple of times a year. Within just a few hundred square feet, at least half a dozen different stations offer pictures, movable pieces, sounds, dress-up, and stories. Just the plastic food can keep a child busy for quite a while. In addition to exhibits, Kidzu offers programs such as story time, and art and crafts projects. Occasionally, visits from artists and people from the community provide enrichment for, or fill the gaps between, exhibits. Admission is good for the entire day, so you can leave for lunch or a break and return later.

Children can explore and learn at their own pace and interest, going from area to area and back again as suits them. Smiling, benevolent volunteers wander through, replacing forgotten objects back to their original place, or restocking paper for drawing, so that when the next child—or the same child—comes through, it's ready.

In the Tot Spot, babies and toddlers may play happily while older siblings explore the exhibit. The padded play area is surrounded by a little fence as well as rocking chairs and bins of books. A "tasted toy" bin in the corner keeps germs in check.

A small gift shop is tucked behind the main desk and has some unusual items related to the exhibit as well as nice toys, accessories, and of course, books. Plans are in the works for Kidzu eventually to move into a larger space, which will make the experience at this museum even better.

Hours: Tuesday through Saturday 10am - 5pm, Sunday 1pm - 5pm. Closed Monday.

Contact Info:

Phone: (919) 933-1455
Website: www.kidzuchildrensmuseum.org
Street address: 105 East Franklin Street, Chapel Hill

Bathrooms: yes
Stroller-friendly: yes, though the museum can get crowded
Food nearby: yes
Picnic-friendly: no
Recommended ages: 2+

Cost: $4 per person. Children 24 months and younger free. Memberships and group rates available.

Morehead Planetarium and Science Center

UNC's planetarium, a gift of alumnus Motley Morehead III, began in 1949 with a projector and one presentation. Today it has many shows, demonstrations, movies, and exhibits, as well as summer camps and programs for children.

About a dozen shows focus on stars, of course, as well as weather and extinction of the dinosaurs. At least one is suitable for preschoolers, and some are seasonal. Science 360, a series about the latest scientific questions, features not only visual media but also discussion between an expert and the audience. Science Live demonstrates topics in science with live experiments and friendly, enthusiastic presenters. Two exhibits and film biographies of influential scientists are included in the planetarium admission. Reservations are required for groups over twenty people, and tickets go on sale thirty minutes before show time.

The planetarium has good summer camps for children preschool-aged and older which combine learning about scientific topics with crafts, activities, and games. During the school year, there are monthly story times for four- to six-year-olds, "Meet the Scientist," and a weekly science club for middle school students.

The gift shop, though small, has space-themed toys and kits, bracelets, fine jewelry, UNC souvenirs, and mood rings. The sundial and rose garden outside appeal to children, who like to run along the paths and walk around the embedded letters.

Hours: Monday through Thursday 10am - 5pm, Friday and Saturday 10am - 5pm and 6:30pm - 9pm, Sunday 1pm - 5pm. Office, Monday through Friday 9am - 5pm. Closed Thanksgiving Day, Christmas Eve, and Christmas Day.

Contact Info:
Phone: (919) 549-6863 information hotline, (919) 962-1236 office and reservations, (919) 843-7997 ticket office and gift shop.
Website: www.moreheadplanetarium.org
Street address: 250 East Franklin Street, Chapel Hill

Bathrooms: yes
Stroller-friendly: yes
Food nearby: yes
Picnic-friendly: not inside, but the campus and rose garden have places to sit
Recommended ages: 6 and up

Cost: adults $6, $5 children 3-12, students, and senior citizens 60+; $2 for second or more shows on the same day. Exhibits and NASA digital theater, free.

Orange County Public Library

Hillsborough's library has occupied the former Orange High School building for many years, and while architecturally historical, the space has become too small for the library. In 2006 the town board approved plans for a new library building, with two stories and over twenty-thousand square feet of space, on the southern edge of the historic downtown. This new location promises to put library patrons within walking distance of shops, restaurants, and the scenic Eno River.

Until then, the library continues to be a cozy, friendly source of books, many periodicals, audio books, and DVDs. The book collection has many titles, especially in the children's and young adult sections, not found elsewhere. If there's a subject or author of particular interest, it's worth checking here.

The children's section is good, too, especially for wholesome books of a higher reading level, so even accelerated readers can find books appropriate for their age, without having to turn to books with themes meant for older children. New books are easily accessible, and easy readers are clearly labeled. When this library moves into its new location, children should be able to stretch out a bit more, though the coziness of the current space has a certain appeal. Add to all of this the friendly, helpful librarians, and you have a great place to stop in Hillsborough.

Hours: Monday through Thursday 9am - 8pm, Friday and Saturday 9am - 5pm, Sunday 1pm - 5pm. Closed holidays.

Contact Info:
Phone: (919) 245-2525
Website: www.co.orange.nc.us/library/orange
Street address: 300 West Tryon Street, Hillsborough

Bathrooms: yes
Stroller-friendly: yes
Food nearby: no
Picnic-friendly: no
Recommended ages: any

Cost: free

Pittsboro Memorial Library/ Chatham Community Library

The Pittsboro Memorial Library, while small, has big plans. Chatham County has approved plans for a new "green" library, nearly five times larger than the current structure, with more features for children and teens, improved access, and better technology. Its new location, on the Central Carolina Community College, with an entrance planned off highway 87, will bring people and events together from all over the community. Under the new name Chatham Community Library, it will better serve the diverse and growing population of Pittsboro, the community college, and the surrounding areas.

Already things are changing. The library has a children's specialist, and the children's section offers activities, story-times, and a summer reading program. In addition to books, there is a good selection of children's videos. With the expansion into the new location, this library will be an excellent resource for education and enrichment.

Hours: Monday, Wednesday, Thursday, and Friday 10am – 6pm, Tuesday 10am – 8pm, Saturday 9am – 5pm. Closed Sunday. Closed on holidays.

Contact Info:
Phone: (919) 542-3524
Website: www.pittsborolibraryfriends.org/index.html, www.chathamnc.org/Index.aspx?page=798
Street Address: 158 West Street, Pittsboro

Bathrooms: yes
Stroller-friendly: yes
Food nearby: yes
Picnic-friendly: no
Recommended ages: any

Cost: free

Revolutionary War Living History Day

Every February, the Alliance for Historic Hillsborough holds Revolutionary War Living History Day, with tours and re-enactments of Cornwallis's Hillsborough encampment in February of 1781. Visitors can see costumed re-enactors cook, drill, march, fire muskets, and even practice medicine in a hospital camp. Two guided tours of historic Revolutionary sites are available during the day with the purchase of a ticket, available in the Dickson House.

Hours: last Saturday in February, 10am - 4pm

Contact Info:
Phone: (919) 732-7741 or (877) 732-7748
Website: www.historichillsborough.org
Street address: Alexander Dickson House, 150 East King Street, Hillsborough

Bathrooms: yes
Stroller-friendly: yes
Food nearby: yes
Picnic-friendly: yes
Recommended ages: any, but especially 5 and up

Cost: $5 per tour ticket

The Twelve Days of Christmas at the Carolina Inn

Every December it's fun to ride the bus into campus to see the Twelve Days of Christmas display in the lobby and halls of the Carolina Inn. Outside the entrance stands a sand sculpture by local artist Sandy Foot. Inside, gorgeous ribbons and garland drape a tall cage holding two live turtledoves that return to the Carolina Inn every year. Down the hall in either direction await artistic renderings of the song's verses amidst all the beauty and grandeur of the Inn. The children like to find the interpretations of twelve lords a-leapin' or five golden rings. In late December, the gingerbread house competition entries are on display at the end of the hall. The works range from cute to astounding as amateurs and professionals create art with gingerbread, frosting, and candy. Viewing the decorations of the Twelve Days of Christmas invokes the spirit of the season, making this a calm, easy outing at an exciting time of year.

Hours: beginning of December through first week of January

Contact Info:

Phone: (919) 933-2001 or (800) 962-8519
Website: www.carolinainn.com
Street address: 211 Pittsboro Street, Chapel Hill

Bathrooms: yes
Stroller-friendly: yes
Food nearby: yes
Picnic-friendly: no
Recommended ages: any, although kids 5 and older may enjoy it more

Cost: free

Part 2: Mostly Outdoors

Festivals

First Sundays in Pittsboro

Every first Sunday of the month, downtown Pittsboro has a local crafts festival with anything from jewelry, pottery, and paintings to cookware, baby accessories, wood furniture, and leatherwork. Restaurants and churches sell food such as baked goods, hot dogs, fish, and funnel cakes. While local non-profits and community organizations field informational booths, artists and artisans display their wares, and some stores and restaurants are open for business. The Chatham Historical Museum is also open, from noon to 4pm. A low-key way to spend a Sunday afternoon, this street fair is a great introduction to the community and wealth of creativity in Chatham County.

Hours: first Sunday of the month, 12pm - 4pm

Contact Info:
Website: www.pittsboroshops.com/FirstSunday.htm
Street address: Hillsboro Street, Pittsboro

Bathrooms: some restaurants and shops open—some have restrooms for the public
Stroller-friendly: yes
Food nearby: yes
Picnic-friendly: no
Recommended ages: any

Cost: free

GrassRoots Festival, Shakori Hills

Shakori Hills, a century-old farm of 75 acres in Chatham county, hosts live music, workshops, festivals, camps, and classes, and most notably the popular GrassRoots Festival, held over four days in April and October. You can go for the day or camp for the whole weekend, but either way you'll have a great time and hear great music. An alternative to the big, commercial amphitheaters, this festival has become popular with bands, most notably Donna the Buffalo, and everything from world music to bluegrass. Its eclectic mix draws an amiable, laid-back, generally progressive crowd. There are also craft vendors, healing arts practitioners, fiddle contests, poetry slams, and environmental and agricultural demonstrations and workshops. For children, well-designed and well-supervised activities include bubbles, face-painting, crafts, story-telling, and children's performances.

Camping is free, but arrive early for a good spot. Cars holding fewer than four people must pay a parking fee. You can bring a picnic and any beverages you (discreetly) enjoy, or buy food and non-alcoholic drinks at the festival. Dress for the weather—nights can still get quite cool at these times of year, and, as it usually rains at least once during the festival, prepare for mud. Bring bug spray and sunscreen and rock out in the casual, convivial atmosphere and best of local and nationally-known musical acts.

Hours: April and October, Thursday 10am - midnight, Friday 9am - 1am, Saturday 9am - midnight, Sunday 9am - 8pm.

Contact Info:
Phone: (919) 542-8142
Website: www.shakorihills.org
Street address: 1439 Henderson Tanyard Road, Pittsboro

Bathrooms: yes
Stroller-friendly: yes, though jog stroller recommended on uneven terrain
Food nearby: yes
Picnic friendly: yes
Recommended ages: any

Cost: 4 day pass, $60-80 per adult, single day pass, $24-34. Discount for children 13-15. Children under 12 free.

Greek Festival

A fundraiser of St. Barbara's Greek Orthodox Church, this local Greek festival has everything Greek: music, icons, books, T-shirts, toys, and fabulous food. Save room for the desserts, which comprise a table of their own. Then sit and enjoy the dancing, scheduled throughout the weekend. The Greek dancers span all ages, and the youngest ones are adorable to watch. After their performances, the dancers invite all to join them. Its good-natured community feeling makes this festival one of the year's highlights.

Hours: first weekend in May, Friday 6pm - 9pm, Saturday 11am - 9pm, Sunday 11am - 8pm

Contact Info:
Website: www.stbarbaraschurch.org/events.htm
Street address: East Chapel Hill High School, 500 Weaver Dairy Road, Chapel Hill

Bathrooms: yes
Stroller-friendly: yes
Food nearby: yes
Picnic-friendly: yes
Recommended ages: any

Cost: $1 admission per person

Carrboro Day

When Carrboro turns out to celebrate, the result is old-fashioned family fun. Bring a picnic blanket or chairs and enjoy the live music, storytelling, and magic shows. Children can make crafts, play games, or take a quiet moment playing in the sand box or blowing bubbles. Parents and children line up for family games such as sack races and balloon toss. The fire department, EMT, and police have tours and demonstrations, sometimes even a new police car open for viewing. Community groups, such as the Carrboro radio station and the public works department, have tables for information or fund-raising. The Carrboro Library often hosts a bake sale to raise money toward building a free-standing library, and concessions such as hot dogs and pizza are also available.

Hours: first Sunday in May, 12:30pm - 7pm

Contact Info:

Phone: (919) 918-7364 Carrboro Recreation and Parks Department
Website: www.carrboro.com/carrboroday
Street address: Town Commons, 301 West Main Street, Carrboro. Rain site: Carrboro Century Center, 100 North Greensboro Street, Carrboro

Bathrooms: yes
Stroller-friendly: yes
Food nearby: yes
Picnic-friendly: yes
Recommended ages: any

Cost: free

Haw River Festival (see also Farms and Nature)

On a Saturday afternoon in May for the past twenty-five years people have gathered in Bynum to learn about, support, and celebrate the Haw River, its people and traditions. Bynum, a once-thriving mill village along the Haw's banks, makes a fitting setting, with its charming mill houses from a time when the river powered the town's economy. The bridge, built circa 1920, was converted to foot traffic in the 1990s, and the mill was shuttered many years before that.

The Haw River Assembly presents this festival every year to raise awareness (and money) and draws a good crowd of artists and musicians. Puppet shows, performances, and arts and crafts keep children entertained. Visual art particularly captures the spirit of the celebration, in large part because of longtime contributions by Bynum resident Clyde Jones, whose annual T-shirt designs are prized by locals and river enthusiasts alike. Clyde leads art projects in many area elementary schools, and his house just up the hill is a great stop for children. His yard, as indeed much of Bynum, is full of his "critters" with tennis ball eyes and glitter paint hides.

Activities vary, but art projects are likely, as well as educational demonstrations. Local organizations sell food, and a raffle and auction occur at the end of the day. The close tie of art, nature, and small town spirit makes this festival special.

You'll likely find yourself returning for the Bynum General Store's summer front porch music series, or just to check out Clyde's newest artistic additions to his yard. Pick up some barbecue at Allen and Son's just up the road on Highway 15-501.

Hours: second Saturday in May, 1pm - 6pm

Contact Info:
Phone: (919) 542-5790
Website: www.hawriver.org
Street address: old Bynum bridge, foot of Bynum Road, Bynum

Bathrooms: yes
Stroller-friendly: yes
Food nearby: yes
Picnic-friendly: yes
Recommended ages: any

Cost: adults $5, children under 14 $3, babies free

Saxapahaw Farmers' Market (see also Arts, Crafts, and Music)

The friendly, casual farmers' market in Saxapahaw has a small but varied collection of wares, from produce, flowers, and locally raised pork to goods such as honey, cheese, local wine, and preserves. The music and festivities around the farmers' market add to the fun, and the view of the Haw River across the road can't be beat. Go for the community experience, support local farmers, and enjoy a relaxed summer evening.

Hours: May through August, Saturday 5pm - 8pm; music begins at 6pm.

Contact Info:
Phone: (336) 376-3122
Website: www.rivermillvillage.com/farmers.html
Street address: 1616 Jordan Drive, Saxapahaw

Bathrooms: yes
Stroller-friendly: yes, though the hill is steep
Food nearby: yes
Picnic-friendly: yes
Recommended ages: any

Cost: donations for the band

Hillsborough Hog Day

Each June, downtown Hillsborough becomes *the* place for North Carolina pork barbecue enthusiasts. Dozens of competitors arrive the night before the event to roast and prepare their pork for the morning's judging. By mid-morning, it's all being chopped up for sale on plates and sandwiches for lunchtime.

While this popular event is founded on the glories of pulled pork, festivities abound. Local music of every genre plays on the stage. Children can take pony rides, play games, and see animals, clowns, puppet shows, and performances on the children's stage. Vendors sell handmade crafts and items of interest. Local business and organizations have booths, too. So wander around and savor the revelry with a plate of the best barbecue around. Though fun, it can get crowded, so consider arriving early.

Hours: third Saturday in June, 9am to 6pm

Contact Info:
Phone: (919) 732-8156 Hillsborough/ Orange County Chamber of Commerce
Website: www.hogdays.com
Street address: downtown Hillsborough

Bathrooms: yes
Stroller-friendly: yes
Food nearby: yes
Picnic-friendly:
Recommended ages: any

Cost: $3 per person, kids 12 and under free

Carrboro 4th of July Celebration

Start celebrating Independence Day in the morning in Carrboro. You can listen to the excellent Village Band play patriotic pieces under the oak trees in front of Town Hall, or meet early at Weaver Street Market to adorn trikes, bikes, strollers, and dogs with red, white, and blue decorations. At ten o'clock, anyone can join the People's Parade and process down Weaver Street to the Town Commons.

Between the Farmers' Market area and Town Hall are tables and booths promoting anything from building a structure for the Carrboro library to political sentiments of usually a liberal stripe. But we walk on past these, unless they're selling brownies and lemonade, to watch the Cane Creek Cloggers dance on stage as the audience whoops and claps. All afternoon, a full schedule of dancers and musical acts keeps the stage area hopping.

Other activities offer entertainment and hometown fun. Despite the heat and sunshine, plenty of people line up for the sack races, watermelon-seed-spitting contest, water-balloon toss, or the funny baby crawl race. The Scrap Exchange has long tables of materials for making your own Independence Day art, with materials like red Styrofoam and silver foil. A long wall stands at the far end of the Commons, where, every year, everyone can paint a square of the wooden quilt. When the heat gets to be too much, a quick stop in the mist tent brings relief.

If you want to buy drinks, slushies, or food, get in line early, as the lines get long fast. The music goes on all day, but we head home when we're weary, happy to have seen some friends, ready to rest up before the evening's fireworks.

Hours: July 4, 11am; parade begins at 10am

Contact Info:
Phone: (919) 942-8541
Website: www.carrboro.com/july4/
Street address: Town Commons, 301 West Main Street, Carrboro

Bathrooms: yes
Stroller-friendly: yes
Food nearby: yes
Picnic-friendly: yes
Recommended ages: any

Cost: free

Chapel Hill 4th of July Celebration

Chapel Hill's Fourth of July Celebration takes place around 7pm in Kenan Stadium on the UNC campus. They've put buildings on all the close parking lots, so the town recommends parking in the Craig and hospital parking lots along Manning Drive and then walking to the stadium. Some disabled parking is available in the adjacent Bell Tower lot.

The doors open at 6:30pm, music by a local band or two starts around 7pm, and the fireworks start around 9:30pm. The fireworks explode low over the stadium, which is problematic in two ways. Inside the stadium, it is not unusual to have cinders fall on the audience. It's too loud and intense for some children, and, frankly, this adult. Outside the stadium, because of the topography and buildings on campus, you need to be very close to the stadium to see any but the highest fireworks. In recent years, you could command a pretty good view from the hospital area, but as construction continues, this could change. The crowds and traffic are terrible, but it's worth it, and anyway, complaining about these is an American tradition you can share with your fellow citizens as you file on home.

Hours: July 4, doors open at 6:30pm, fireworks 9 or 9:30pm

Contact Info:
Phone: (919) 968-2784 Chapel Hill Parks and Recreation Department
Website: www.townofchapelhill.org/index.asp?NID=1042
Street address: 201 Stadium Drive, UNC Campus, Chapel Hill

Bathrooms: yes
Stroller-friendly: yes
Food nearby: yes
Picnic-friendly: outside the stadium
Recommended ages: any, but it can get intense and crowded inside the stadium

Cost: free

Family Fun Day in Hillsborough

This being Hillsborough, the annual Family Fun Day has not only food and vendors, but also historic guided tours and artisan demonstrations. The farmers' market is open, and there are activities for children. Start at the Orange County Visitor's Center for a map and list of activities.

Hours: first Saturday in July, 10am - 4pm

Contact Info:
Phone: (919) 732-7741 or (877) 732-7748
Website: www.historichillsborough.org
Street address: Orange County Visitor's Center, 150 East King Street, Hillsborough

Bathrooms: yes
Stroller-friendly: yes
Food nearby: yes
Picnic-friendly: yes
Recommended ages: any

Cost: free

Chatham County Fair

This local fair is smaller and friendlier than the State Fair, with much shorter lines. You'll see demonstrations on everything from cider-making and cow-milking to carpentry and manicures. Entertainment includes performances by church and gospel choirs and dance groups. Competitions in spelling and dancing add spice, and games such as egg-carrying and sack races are as much fun to watch as participate in. Of course, no fair would be complete without rides and cotton candy. Check the websites for exact dates and admission prices.

Hours: second week in September, starts on Wednesday evening and runs through the weekend

Contact Info:
Phone: (919) 542-8200 Chatham County government
Website: www.ncfairs.org, www.chathamnc.org
Street address: Martin Luther King Drive, Pittsboro (behind the Food Lion)

Bathrooms: yes
Stroller-friendly: yes
Food nearby: yes
Picnic-friendly: yes
Recommended ages: any

Cost: varies

Fiesta de la Familia

Unlike the enormous (though exciting) Fiesta del Pueblo in Raleigh, this celebration of Hispanic culture is a manageable size, for less stress and more fun for the whole family. Children can make crafts and play, and everyone can enjoy the colorful dancing, live music, food, and art from countries all over Central and South America, as citizens of any origin come to experience this expression of the richness of Carrboro's community.

Hours: mid-September, 1pm - 6pm

Contact Info:

Phone: (919) 932-4652 El Centro of Carrboro
Website: www.elcentrolatino.org
Street address: Town Commons, 301 West Main Street, Carrboro

Bathrooms: no
Stroller-friendly: yes
Food nearby: yes
Picnic-friendly: yes
Recommended ages: any

Cost: free

Celebration of the Automobile Car Show

Hillsborough's Historic Speedway group holds this annual event to raise funds to restore and preserve the Occoneechi Orange Speedway, built in 1949 and one of the first NASCAR racetracks. You will see lots and lots of cars, over 400 of them: antique cars, stock cars, historic race cars, all kinds of cars, many with the hoods up so visitors can admire the engines. Race drivers, car restorers, and car enthusiasts share stories and visit. Vendors and organizations sell such concessions as pizza and baked goods. There are contests, live music, and speakers. The Speedway's oval track, now filled with woods, makes an excellent place for a family hike. It is one of only three racetracks on the National Register of Historic Places (Indianapolis Speedway is one of the other two)—definitely a worthy cause and fun for the whole family.

Hours: last Saturday in September, 8am - 5pm

Contact Info:
Phone: (919) 918-7364
Website: www.historicspeedway.org
Street address: 320 Elizabeth Brady Road, Hillsborough

Bathrooms: yes
Stroller-friendly: yes
Food nearby: yes
Picnic-friendly: yes
Recommended ages: any

Cost: free

Carrboro Music Festival

In 1998, some music-minded citizens decided to create a free music festival in Carrboro to showcase the well-known local music community. At first, the Carrboro Music Festival began as part of the French summer solstice celebration, Fête de la Musique, in June. Unfortunately, Carrboro in the summer is hot, and, with the university and schools out, largely empty. So, after a few years, the festival became independent of the French holiday, and moved to the more favorable atmosphere of September.

With over 150 musical acts playing all over town, just pushing the stroller down the street past blue grass playing from the porch of one store, towards the sounds of reggae or jazz behind a restaurant, can be a very cool experience. Children dancing in public is practically the hallmark of Carrboro, and some shows are quite family-friendly. Schedules and descriptions of performers are available online and in local newspapers. The town gets rather crowded, so visitors can park in the back lot of Carrboro Plaza and catch the free shuttle bus into town.

Hours: last Sunday in September, begins at 1 pm

Contact Info:
Website: carrboromusicfestival.com
Street Address: downtown Carrboro

Bathrooms: yes, at some venues
Stroller-friendly: yes
Food nearby: yes
Picnic-friendly: yes
Recommended ages: any

Cost: free

Festifall

Chapel Hill's arts and crafts street fair began in 1972, and, while much bigger today, you are likely to see people you know as you wander past vendors, booths, music, and dancing. The crafts range from pottery and painting to clothing and woodworking. Non-profit and town services also have informational booths. The food vendors are as many and varied as downtown itself. Performances include live music from local musicians of every stripe, the Apple Chill Cloggers, teen and cultural dance groups, and martial arts demonstrations. You'll also find inflatable bouncy structures, activities, and performances for children. Despite the outdoor venue, pets are not allowed at Festifall.

Hours: first Sunday in October, 1pm - 6pm

Contact Info:
Phone: (919) 968-2784 Chapel Hill Parks and Recreation Department
Website: www.festifall.com,www.chapelhillparks.org
Street address: downtown Franklin Street, Chapel Hill

Bathrooms: yes
Stroller-friendly: yes
Food nearby: yes
Picnic-friendly: yes—on the nearby UNC quad McCorkle Place
Recommended ages: any

Cost: free

The Pumpkin Run

What other running event serves pumpkin pie, *with* whipped cream, and, instead of customary T-shirts, awards *socks*, with a different design every year, to every participant? The Pumpkin Run is a special event, both playful—many participants run in Halloween costumes, once including the seven dwarves—and good for the soul. The women's running group seejanerun founded this 4K race in part to celebrate the beautiful wooded course in Carolina North Forest. The five o'clock starting time captures these woods in the golden October light. It also accommodates families' busy Saturday schedules. Kids as young as six like participating, although the hilly terrain may have them walking quite a bit. No matter. Finishing is what counts here, and like all great races, at the Pumpkin Run, every runner is cheered to the finish line.

Afterwards, everyone heads to the party for pizza, pumpkin pie, and water, cider, or other beverages. Then the games begin: a push-up competition, jump-roping, line dancing, and fellowship. In 2007 the Chapel Hill-Carrboro YMCA hosted the race and party, but details change, so check the website, and sign up early, as the popularity of this race grows every year. It's a great family activity with lots of healthy fun.

Hours: Saturday before Halloween, 5pm

Contact Info:
Website: www.pumpkin.runningland.com
Street address: Race course is at the end of Municipal Drive, off Martin Luther King Jr. Boulevard, Chapel Hill

Bathrooms: yes
Stroller-friendly: at the party only—no strollers permitted in the race
Food nearby: yes
Picnic-friendly: yes
Recommended ages: 6 and up

Cost: $25 per participant

Pittsboro Street Fair

While small, this arts and crafts fair makes a satisfying outing on a fall day. Non-profits and community service organizations field tables with information, games, raffles, and items for sale. Entertainers such as animal-balloon wielding clowns stroll through the crowd. For a fee, children can jump in various inflatable bouncy structures. Food vendors and live music add to the festivities.

Hours: last Saturday in October, 10am - 5pm

Contact Info:

Phone: (919) 545-8555 Chatham County Parks and Recreation Department
Street Address: Hanks Street, west of Hillsboro Street, near southern end of Credle Street

Bathrooms: no
Stroller-friendly: yes
Food nearby: yes
Picnic-friendly: no
Recommended ages: any

Cost: free

ARTS, CRAFTS, AND MUSIC

The ArtsCenter

This not-for-profit organization offers classes, art exhibits, musical and theatrical performances, and programs for adults and children. The popular Super Fun Shows are reliably kid-friendly, with lots of humor and audience participation. It is worth getting on the ArtsCenter e-mail list to find out which shows are coming up so you can plan ahead. Getting tickets even the day of the show is usually not a problem—a call to the knowledgeable box office staff can help you decide—but you'll want to arrive in plenty of time to get a seat with a view for the little ones. Though the theater's design can be a bit frustrating, children's performers do make a point of addressing or even walking around all the seating sections, so no seat is too far from the action.

The ArtsCenter also offers a variety of classes in arts and crafts. The ArtsCenter Youth division offers shows, a theatre program, and many summer and after-school classes and camps. The ArtSchool, the education wing of the ArtsCenter, has courses for adults and children, in such areas as dance, pottery, music, art exploration, and even sewing. Classes involve plenty of hands-on opportunities, and projects are well-suited to the age of the students. While the ArtsCenter courses tend to be a bit more expensive than other recreation programs, their instructors are excellent, often locally recognized experts in their fields and experienced teachers.

Hours: box office, Monday through Friday 10am - 6pm, Saturday 12pm - 4pm

Contact Info:
Phone: (919) 929-2787 administrative offices, (919) 929-2787, ext. 201 box office
Website: www.artscenterlive.org
Street address: 300-G East Main Street, Carrboro

Bathrooms: yes
Stroller-friendly: yes
Food nearby: yes
Picnic-friendly: no
Recommended ages: toddlers and up

Cost: varies

Bynum Front Porch Series

Motorists hurtling across Highway 15-501 bridge over the Haw River may note the old dam a hundred yards or so north, but few, unless they are native to the area—or local art or music enthusiasts—are likely to know about the town of Bynum that lies a half mile downstream. The heart of this former mill town is the Bynum General Store and post office, which had to close a few years back due to lack of business. Recently, the community rallied to preserve this historic site with a local music series that features great, even nationally-known musicians. The outdoor stage stands next to the General Store there on Bynum Road, and vendors sell food and non-alcoholic beverages.

Hours: Fridays, May through September, 7pm

Contact Info:

Phone: (919) 542-0394 Chatham County Arts Council
Website: bynumfrontporch.googlepages.com
Street address: 950 Bynum Road, Bynum

Bathrooms: yes
Stroller-friendly: yes
Food nearby: yes
Picnic-friendly: no
Recommended ages: any

Cost: $3-7 suggested donation for the band

Chatham Marketplace

Located in the restored historic mill near downtown, Chatham Marketplace is Pittsboro's cooperative grocery store. The café corner inside is a cozy space for eating some of the store's delicious food or meeting with friends. Outside, porch has tables and toys, and on the lawn, tables, chairs, and plenty of grass provide a welcome place to relax. Events throughout the week include beer tastings, classes in cooking or soap-making, poetry readings, book signings, and live music. The Sunday Brunch music series features local and well-known musicians, and takes place rain or shine. The atmosphere is positive and community-friendly, making a pleasant place to enjoy a quiet morning or a lively event.

Hours: daily 8am - 8pm

Contact Info:
Phone: (919) 542-2643
Website: www.chathammarketplace.coop
Street address: 480 Hillsboro Street, Pittsboro

Bathrooms: yes
Stroller-friendly: yes
Food nearby: yes
Picnic-friendly: yes
Recommended ages: any

Cost: free; donations for band

Cool Jazz Festival

All day long, on two stages, both well-known musicians and local and high school groups perform jazz. There's plenty of food, arts, and crafts for sale as well. Bring chairs or picnic blanket and enjoy one of the area's few music festivals to focus solely on jazz. The series continues on selected Thursday nights at 8pm.

Hours: Saturday in April, 9am – 7pm

Contact Info:
Phone: (919) 245-2660 Orange County Recreation and Parks
Website: www.co.orange.nc.us/recparks/jazz_fest.asp
Street address: New Hope Park, Highway 86 near New Hope Church Road, Hillsborough. Rain site: Orange High School, Hillsborough

Bathrooms: yes
Stroller-friendly: yes
Food nearby: yes
Picnic-friendly: yes
Recommended ages: any

Cost: free; parking $5 per car

Last Fridays in Hillsborough

Discover the artistic scene in Hillsborough on the old courthouse lawn downtown as live music plays and local artists and artisans set up tables with their works, from pottery to jewelry, along the sidewalk. Businesses, galleries, and museums open their doors for visitors to see exhibits of paintings and other visual arts. In cooler weather, the focus turns indoors, to theater and film in addition to music. Food and activities lend fun to the festivities.

Hours: last Friday of the month, April through September, 6pm - 9pm

Contact Info:

Phone: (919) 643-2500 Hillsborough Arts Council
Websites: www.hillsboroughartscouncil.org/Last_Fridays.html
Street address: Hillsborough Artists Co-operative, 102 West King Street, Hillsborough

Bathrooms: yes
Stroller-friendly: yes
Food nearby: yes
Picnic-friendly: yes
Recommended ages: all

Cost: varies

Lincoln Arts Center

For years, the Lincoln Arts Center occupied a large, airy room adjacent to the Chapel Hill-Carrboro City Schools administration building. When the school system requested the use of the space, the town of Chapel Hill began looking for a new home for the studio.

The new location is in the garage of the Chapel Hill Parks and Recreation office, where, under a new name, the studio will continue to host classes in wheel and hand pottery, painting, and general art classes designed to encourage and develop children's artistic expression. The instructors tend to be skilled, enthusiastic, and supportive.

Hours: varies by class

Contact Information:

Phone: (919) 968-2784 Chapel Hill Parks and Recreation Department
Website: www.ci.chapel-hill.nc.us/index.asp?NID=68
Street address: Lincoln Arts Center, 750 South Merritt Mill Road, Chapel Hill.; new studio, 200 Plant Road, Chapel Hill

Bathrooms: yes
Stroller-friendly: yes
Food nearby: no
Picnic-friendly: yes, at nearby Community Center
Recommended ages: preschool and up

Cost: varies

Occaneechi-Saponi Spring Festival and Pow Wow

This Native American event is a colorful, musical celebration of the crafts and traditions of this local tribe, with storytelling, singing, and dancing. Booths feature artifacts as well as handcrafted dream-catchers, silver and gold artwork, leatherworking, and woodworking. The eventual completion of a cultural center on the tribal lands will offer exhibits, classes and demonstrations for visitors to learn more about this tribe's interesting and complex history. The tribal grounds include the reconstruction of an Occaneechi Village from 1701, with a fire ring, buildings, and gardens, replicating how the tribe used to live. Groups may call ahead to schedule a tour.

Hours: early to mid-June, Friday 5pm - 9pm, Saturday 10am - 9pm

Contact Info:
Phone: (919) 304-3723 or (919) 732-8512
Website: www.occaneechi-saponi.org
Street address: Occaneechi Tribal Grounds, 4902 Daily Store Road, Burlington

Bathrooms: yes
Stroller-friendly: yes
Food nearby: yes
Picnic-friendly: yes
Recommended ages: any

Cost: adults $6, children under 12 and senior citizens, $3

Old-Fashioned Farmer's Day

This festival, the longest running in Chatham County, celebrates the farming history, culture, and community. Agricultural demonstrations run the gamut, from saw milling, rock crushing, and baling to sheep-herding dogs and molasses-making. Anticipate plenty of history, too, with displays of antique tractors, equipment, and methods. Children will enjoy the farm animals, pony rides, inflatable bouncy structures, and homemade ice cream. There's barbecue and all kinds of homemade food and desserts. Vendors offer such items as pottery, and local churches sell crafts. Entertainment includes contests, live bluegrass music, gospel performances, and folk dancing. Proceeds go to local charitable causes. Dogs on leashes are permitted, except near where food is sold.

Hours: first weekend in September, opens 6pm Friday, 9am Saturday and Sunday

Contact Info:
Phone: (919) 742-4881
Website: www.silkhoperuritans.com, www.visitchathamcounty.com
Street address: G.T. Petty Memorial Fairgrounds, Silk Hope Road, Siler City

Bathrooms: yes
Stroller-friendly: yes
Food nearby: yes
Picnic-friendly: yes
Recommended ages: any

Cost: $5

Paperhand Puppet Intervention

Paperhand Puppet Intervention is a group of artists committed to puppetry and making the world a better place. Their performances are amazing as the big, artistic puppets glide around, manipulated with poles. Audiences are comprised largely of children and families. Before the show, they have music and dancing, just for fun. The performances include audience participation, and the performers walk the puppets through the crowd.

Seeing their show at UNC's Forest Theatre is a special treat. The outdoor stone amphitheater makes it an adventure—though a dusty one. Bring blankets or sit-upons and enjoy a picnic. Parking is very limited, so you may want to get a ride, especially on game nights, when traffic will be bad. At places such as the ArtsCenter, picnics are not allowed, though food is available in nearby downtown Carrboro; on the other hand, such venues have nicer bathrooms.

The group also holds workshops and participates in parades such as Carrboro's July 4th parade and First Night in Raleigh. With their gentle, giant artistry, Paperhand Puppet Intervention is practically a Chapel Hill institution.

Hours: varies by venue; pre-show starts half an hour before performance time

Contact Info:
Phone: (919) 923-1857
Website: www.paperhand.org
Street address: varies

Bathrooms: depends on venue
Stroller-friendly: yes
Food nearby: depends on venue
Picnic-friendly: yes
Recommended ages: any

Cost: varies; at Forest Theatre, $10 adults, $7 children, free for children 3 and under

Saturdays in Saxapahaw Rivermill Music Series

We have been lucky enough to see such great groups as the Carolina Chocolate Drops just before they became popular, here at the Saxapahaw music series. This event is casual and comfortable, in part because all the children are busy playing on the enormous slip-and-slide, riding the kayak-zip-line, getting their faces painted, or participating in some other kid-friendly activity provided by CERES, a local organization. The hillside slope above the stage is pleasantly shaded, and the view of the mill and river just beyond is fabulous. The farmers' market, though small, has vendors for local wine, baked goods, honey, and flowers.

Hours: May through August, Saturday 5pm - 8pm; music begins at 6pm

Contact Info:
Phone: (336) 376-5694 Saxapahaw Rivermill events and press information
Website: www.rivermillvillage.com/satinsax.html
Street address: 1616 Jordan Drive, Saxapahaw

Bathrooms: yes
Stroller-friendly: yes, though the hill is steep
Food nearby: yes
Picnic-friendly: yes
Recommended ages: any

Cost: free; donations for band

Shakori Hills Summer Outdoor Music Series

Smaller than the Grassroots Festival, the Moonlight, Music, and Dance events have the same laid-back atmosphere of the Shakori Hills farm. Pizza is available, and local farmers and crafters sell their wares. Children flock together and run around the pretty farm, and adults enjoy beer or wine and great music. Shakori Hills can have its pick of the best musical acts around, so bring the kids, a picnic, some bug spray, and your dancing shoes.

Hours: first Saturday of the month, May through October, 6:30pm - 10pm; music begins at 7:30pm

Contact Info:
Phone: (919) 542-8142
Website: www.shakorihills.org
Street address: 1439 Henderson Tanyard Road, Pittsboro

Bathrooms: yes
Stroller-friendly: yes
Food nearby: yes
Picnic-friendly: yes
Recommended ages: any

Cost: suggested donation of $5 - $8 per adult

Weaver Street Market

Since this cooperative grocery store opened in 1987, it has become a local gathering place for students, retirees, families, everyone in between, and their dog. The shaded lawn feels like an oasis in the heart of bustling downtown Carrboro. The big oak tree has irresistible roots just made for stepping around, and the crepe myrtles and rock fountain are perfect for exploring or resting. Find a table or spot on the grass, add delicious bread and some items from the deli bar, and call it a perfect day. Keep an eye on children playing, however, for only a thin border of bushes separates the lawn from the traffic of Weaver Street.

During the warm months, the Thursday After Hours and Sunday Jazz & More brunch series feature live music and excellent food for sale, often for a worthy local cause. Either event can get crowded, so arrive early with blanket or chairs, or squeeze next to the friends or acquaintances you're bound to meet here. Throughout the year, storytellers, agricultural demonstrations, and performers appear here as well.

Weaver Street Market has two other stores in the area. In Southern Village, you can eat outside and enjoy the bustle of Market Street. The new store in Hillsborough has the same products and fresh food available at the other stores.

Hours: daily 8am - 9pm. After **Hours:** Thursday 6pm - 8pm. Jazz and More: Sunday 11am - 1pm.

Contact Info:

Phone: (919) 929-0010 Carrboro, (919) 929-2009 Southern Village
Website: www.weaverstreetmarket.coop, www.carrboro.com/wsmjazz.html
Street address: 100 East Weaver Street, Carrboro; 716 Market Street, Chapel Hill; 228 South Churton Street, Hillsborough.

Bathrooms: yes
Stroller-friendly: yes
Food nearby: yes
Picnic-friendly: yes
Recommended ages: any

Cost: free unless you buy food

Fridays on the Front Porch

Rain or shine, the Carolina Inn's front lawn is the stately setting for music and casual dining. Live bluegrass music brings the children to the front to dance. Arrive early if you want a table, for they fill up quickly. Fortunately, there's plenty of room for blankets. Bring a picnic, or enjoy delicious food, such as the best macaroni and cheese and baked beans ever tasted, from the Inn's buffet, complete with adult beverages. A lot of fun, and an elegant variation on the outdoor music scene.

Hours: End of April through September, Fridays, 5pm – 7pm

Contact Info:
Phone: (919) 918-2777
Website: www.carolinainn.com
Street Address: 211 Pittsboro Street, Chapel Hill

Bathrooms: yes
Stroller-friendly: yes
Food nearby: yes
Picnic-friendly: yes
Recommended ages: any

Cost: free; food costs extra

Part 3: Definitely Outdoors

Parks and Playgrounds

Anderson Community Park

This fifty-five acre park lying on the western edge of Carrboro has lots of space for play and repose. The half-mile long gravel nature trail encircling the pond is wide and easy to walk, even for small children, and the ducks and geese happily accept offers of bread.

The playground, farther back in the park, has two play structures, one for toddlers and one for older children. Between the two play areas is a good supply of swings. A small rock-climbing dome provides an excellent place underneath for playing house or hiding. The playground surface consists of mulch, under the larger play structure, and sand everywhere else. Trees surrounding the playground provide welcome shade, and parking is close, handy in case you forget something in the car.

The park also includes playing fields and picnic tables, grills, and shelters available for rent. You can even borrow, for the day, a fishing rod and equipment from the Carrboro Recreation and Parks Department at the Century Center, and go fishing in the pond and enjoy an easy day at the park.

Hours: daily 7am - dark

Contact Info:
Phone: (919) 918-7364 Recreation and Parks, (919) 918-7385 Century Center
Websites: townofcarrboro.org/RP/parks.htm, www.carrboro.com/parks.html
Street address: 302 Hwy 54 West, Carrboro

Bathrooms: yes
Stroller-friendly: yes—though the gravel trail can be a problem for some strollers
Food nearby: no
Picnic-friendly: yes
Recommended ages: any

Cost: free

Carrboro Elementary School Park

Thanks to a diligent PTA, the Carrboro Elementary School Park has some great new play equipment, including a new tree fort for 5 to 7 year-olds, a smaller climbing wall for 7- to 9-year-olds, and a pirate ship for 9 and up with climbing wall, rope ladders, and a ramp. Two little wooden cabins offer an excellent place to play house or restaurant. For purists, there are nine regular swings and one special adaptable swing, and a slide.

Within fencing, the preschool playground has a play structure. Behind it, tucked in the edge of the woods, is the "tree house," a deck for sitting or playing. The basketball courts nearby are good for a game, jumping rope, or whirling a hula hoop. The dirt track beyond is 0.16 mile in length—not too long for little ones.

This playground has a shady side and a sunny side, with plenty of room to run around and picnic tables for rest. The nearby paved bike path is named for Frances Shetley, who saved Carr Mill at the eleventh hour; it leads to Greensboro Street, across the street from Williams Street and the entrance to Wilson Park.

Hours: weekdays, 3pm - dusk; weekends, dawn to dusk

Contact Info:
Phone: (919) 918-7364 Carrboro Recreation and Parks Department
Websites: www.carrboro.com/parks.html, www.ci.carrboro.nc.us/RP/parks.htm
Street address: 400 Shelton Street, Carrboro

Bathrooms: no
Stroller-friendly: yes
Food nearby: no
Picnic-friendly: yes
Recommended ages: any

cost: free

Cedar Falls Park

This large park has trails, courts, a playground, and several athletic fields. Teams from East Chapel Hill High School just across the street sometimes practice here, as do many recreational leagues.

The playground recently received new play equipment, including two play structures, one for children ages 2 to 5, and a larger one for older children. Four swings, two with toddler seats, stand behind the structures and have mats below them, as do the slides. Of particular interest is a stand alone hand-pedaling piece—kids wait in line for a turn with it.

One of the nicest features of this park is the hiking, with 2.5 miles of nature trails. The Jo Peeler trail winds for about half a mile around the park. A self-guide explains the history of the park and trees and plants along the path, but what a preschooler may like are the big rocks to sit on, funny shaped trees, checking the numbers on the post markers, and keeping track of the yellow spots that mark the trail. The blue and white trails are longer, so if your children are older and hardier, they may enjoy exploring more of this oasis within town.

From the playground you can see the ballfields and the six tennis courts. Picnic tables near the playground provide places to rest among the trees and attractions of this popular park.

Hours: dawn to dusk

Contact Info:
Phone: (919) 968-2784 Chapel Hill Parks and Recreation
Website: www.chapelhillparks.org
Street Address: 501 Weaver Dairy Rd, Chapel Hill

Bathrooms: yes
Stroller-friendly: yes, though the natural trails may be unsuitable even for jog strollers
Food nearby: no
Picnic-friendly: yes
Recommended ages: any

Cost: free

Ephesus Park

The school playground has equipment not usually found in public parks and is especially well-suited to children ages five and up. The tennis courts are lighted, and the athletic fields are a popular site for games in warm weather. The park also includes a short nature trail.

Hours: dawn to dusk

Contact Info:
Phone: (919) 968-2784 Chapel Hill Parks and Recreation Department
Website: townhall.townofchapelhill.org/parks_&_rec/facilities_greenways_&_parks
Street address: 1501 Ephesus Church Road, Chapel Hill

Bathrooms: no
Stroller-friendly: yes
Food nearby: no
Picnic-friendly: yes
Recommended ages: any, but especially 5 and up

Cost: free

Hargraves Community Center and Park

This beautiful historic building holds classes, events, and programs for adults and children. There are courts for basketball (indoor and outdoor), tennis, and volleyball.

The playground has been recently updated, with pretty landscaping, fresh mulch, all new play equipment and plenty of innovative ways to climb, hang, slide, and swing. The toddler playground has a puppet theater and play structure, but no swings. A new fence separates the playground from conveniently close parking lots on both sides and a picnic shelter with grills and six tables.

Hours: Playground, dawn to dusk.
Hargraves Center, Monday through Friday 1pm - 9pm, Saturday and Sunday 2pm - 6pm

Contact Info:
Phone: (919) 968-2794
Website: www.ci.chapel-hill.nc.us/index.asp?NID=115
Street address: 216 North Roberson Street, Chapel Hill

Bathrooms: yes
Stroller-friendly: yes
Food nearby: no, though downtown Carrboro is not far
Picnic-friendly: yes
Recommended ages: any

Cost: free

Homestead Park

While parking is not close, the walk to the park, past the dog park and over a pretty bridge, can be interesting. The paved path leads to the playground with the purple double slide. Two friends can race down the slide at the same time, and under the slide's steps is a cozy place for playing. There are swings for both toddlers and older children, and a larger structure suits kids five and older. The natural area surrounding the playground has irresistible boulders, sticks and rocks. Picnic tables can be found in any direction, some in the playground area and others tucked into the woods. With its ample parking and a playground surrounded by a buffer of trees, trails, and tables, this park works well for gatherings and play groups.

Athletic fields sit on either side of the playground. At the far end of the parking lot, the skate park and batting cages have an admission fee and passes available, and the aquatics center is scheduled to open by summer of 2008.

Hours: dawn to dusk

Contact Info:
Phone: (919) 968-2784 Chapel Hill Parks and Recreation Department
Website: townhall.townofchapelhill.org/parks_&_rec/facilities_greenways_&_parks
Street address: 100 Northern Park Drive, off Homestead Road, Chapel Hill

Bathrooms: yes
Stroller-friendly: yes
Food nearby: no
Picnic-friendly: yes
Recommended ages: any

Cost: free

Martin Luther King Jr. Park

A community garden, organized by the Community Garden Coalition, occupies part of the ten acres of Carrboro's newest park. The other part is a multi-purpose field, for now. Future plans include a playground, gardens, outdoor game tables, open play areas, picnic tables, and restrooms.

Hours: dawn to dusk

Contact Info:
Phone: (919) 918-7364 Carrboro Recreation and Parks Department
Website: www.carrboro.com/parks.html, www.ci.carrboro.nc.us/rp/default.htm
Street address: 1120 Hillsborough Road, Carrboro

Bathrooms: no
Stroller-friendly: no
Food nearby: no
Picnic-friendly: yes
Recommended ages: any

Cost: free

Meadowmont Park

Meadowmont Park shares the Rashkis Elementary playground, with all its new play structures and equipment, as well as athletic field and basketball courts. At the end of the parking lot, a picnic shelter overlooks a quiet pond and a log cabin. The mile of paved trail to Highway 54 West begins here, as does a half-mile nature trail to Lancaster Drive. For an outing with friends, this park might be just the place, as nothing is too far away in Meadowmont, including eating establishments and a grocery store.

Hours: dawn to dusk

Contact Info:
Phone: (919) 968-2784 Chapel Hill Parks and Recreation Department
Website: townhall.townofchapelhill.org/parks_&_rec/facilities_greenways_&_parks
Street address: 621 Meadowmont Lane, Chapel Hill

Bathrooms: no
Stroller-friendly: yes
Food nearby: no, but restaurants and businesses are within walking distance
Picnic-friendly: yes
Recommended ages: any, though especially ages 5 and up

Cost: free

Neighborhood Parks

In Chapel Hill and Carrboro, you may find quiet parks and playgrounds tucked into odd corners. While not major destinations like the Community Center or Anderson Park, these small parks provide a meeting place for playdates or a break from the usual. I've included information on surface material because one of my children, as a toddler, seemed compelled to eat mulch, so for about a year I sought parks without it. Few have restrooms, but many are near businesses or restaurants, as noted.

Chapel Hill Parks

townhall.townofchapelhill.org/parks_&_rec/facilities_greenways_&_parks/parks

Burlington Park, Ephesus Church Road

This little park, nestled downhill from a busy road, is surrounded by creeks on one side and a ditch on the other. A small field offers a place to run or practice soccer, or you can run past the old swing sets and over the bridge (pausing only to throw sticks into the water) to the shaded playground with small play structure and bouncy animals on springs. The play structure has no steps, only a ladder, which may be hard for preschoolers or toddlers to manage. Each of the three picnic tables has a charming peaked, shingled roof. There are no bathrooms, and the nearest eating establishment is back at one of the shopping centers off Fordham Boulevard.

Jones Park, Holland Drive

A natural trail leads a half mile through lovely poplar and beech woods typical of North Carolina creekland. The creek itself has interesting inhabitants such as crayfish. The playground has been removed and closed, and the park itself may feel a bit secluded, but if you're stuck in the hospital area, the trail may be a useful diversion, as it connects the park to the Community Church at the corner of Purefoy Road and Mason Farm Road, near the hospital's parking garage.

Oakwood Park, 20 Oakwood Drive

The sand surface and ready supply of sticks from the surrounding trees offer entertainment in themselves, but this playground also has one of the town's few zip-lines—close to the ground and great fun. The good-sized play structure is shaded by trees, though the several swings are in the sun. This playground can be buggy in the summer, so bring repellent. The shade is welcome, and a bench and picnic table by the structure provide places to rest. A chain-link fence separates the playground from the streets, and across the intersection are two tennis courts. Just down the road in either direction, Glen Lennox and Meadowmont have kid-friendly restaurants.

North Forest Hills Park, 121 Collums Road

Though the sign says the playground is designed for 5 to 12 year-olds, even toddlers will enjoy the ramps, slides, and low height of the play structure. Sand covers the ground around the play structure. Hedges divide the play area from the small parking lot, important for those reckless games of chase. Uphill from the playground stands a half-court basketball goal. Below, the path leads to a grassy area about 100 x 50 feet, good for a game of badminton, Frisbee, or chase. The paved paths seem perfect for small bikes or scooters. With six picnic tables and shelter, grills, water fountain, and even bathrooms (open from May through October) this playground would accommodate a playgroup or gathering. The shelter can be reserved through the Chapel Hill Parks and Recreation Department.

Southern Village Playgrounds, Newell Street, Edgewater Drive, and Highgrove Street

Owned and maintained by the Southern Village Homeowners' Association, these cheerful playgrounds have fencing and new play equipment. Benches and picnic tables sit at the edges. They are on or near the trail winding around Southern Village, so you can make an outing of it, if you like.

Westwood Park, Dogwood Drive

You might miss this small park at first, as it sits below the road, sheltered by trees. The play structure and bench sit quietly in this pretty, shaded setting.

Carrboro Parks

townofcarrboro.org/RP/parks.htm

Baldwin Park Park, 400 Broad Street

Baldwin park has a shaded, sloping lawn, a basketball goal, a picnic shelter (without tables), and a playground. The play structure would suit smaller children. A small set of swings stands to one side, but the real draw would be the sand diggers. A footpath leads from the park to the adjoining neighborhood, and downtown Carrboro business district lies only a few blocks' walk away.

Brewer's Lane Park, 102 Hargraves Street

This mini-park has a basketball court and open space.

Simpson Street Park, 301 Simpson Street

Once just a quiet collection of picnic tables under dogwood trees, this gem of a neighborhood park has recently been refurbished with a new, small playground. Parents of reckless toddlers may appreciate the fencing separating the park from the traffic below. One of the swings has a pull-down harness to adapt to children who need a little more stability. The impressive climbing gym offers opportunities to hang and swing. The slide is not too high, and children seem to enjoy the modern interpretation of a see saw that bounces on a large spring. The shade is welcome in summer, and a picnic table and grill to the side give a place to rest from playing. The park might not suit large groups, as parking is limited to the curbs of busy Main Street and narrow Simpson Street, and the park is rather small.

Southern Community Park

Take your children, dogs, bikes, and skates to the newest Chapel Hill town park, located just south of Southern Village and scheduled to open in the summer of 2008. Much of the park's 72 acres will remain natural, with a meadow, dog park, and trails for walking and biking. Althletic fields and courts are due to be completed the following year, so enthusiasts of team sports from softball and basketball to disk golf and inline skate hockey will have something to look forward to.

The park's trail connects to the Southern Village path and Fan Branch trail near Scroggs Elementary. This wide, paved trail leads for a little over half a mile along Fan Branch Creek, skirting the edge of Southern Village, to its conclusion at Culbreth Road. While there are no places to stop along the trail itself, Market Street near Scroggs Elementary has plenty of places to eat or refresh, or even picnic on the lawn. In warm months, the Village Lawn is the site of outdoor movies, live music concerts, a weekly farmers' market, and more.

Hours: dawn to dusk

Contact Info:
Phone: (919) 968-2784 Chapel Hill Parks and Recreation Department
Website: www.townofchapelhill.org/index.asp?NID=1339, townhall.townofchapelhill.org/parks_&_rec/facilities_greenways_&_parks/greenways/fan_branch

Street Address: Hwy 15-501 South and Dogwood Acres Drive, Chapel Hill

Bathrooms: yes
Stroller-friendly: yes
Food nearby: yes
Picnic-friendly: **yes**
Recommended ages: any

Cost: free

Town Commons Park

This playground's play structure, in all its details, is just right for toddlers and preschoolers, with things to turn and look through, little slides, and safe steps for satisfying that toddler urge to climb stairs. A thoughtful group of parents worked to obtain an awning over the playground, for while it is a nice, fenced-in area, with a good, plastic surface, it gets a lot of sun. There's plenty of room to run around outside the playground fence, and benches are nearby for resting and watching. Shops, downtown Carrboro, even the interesting yard full of art at the corner of Poplar and Main, are just a short walk away. During the farmers' market on Saturday mornings and, to a lesser degree, Wednesday afternoons, this playground is a social vortex of happily playing children.

Hours: dawn to dusk

Contact Info:
Phone: (919) 918-7364 Carrboro Recreation and Parks Department
Website: www.carrboro.com/parks.html, www.ci.carrboro.nc.us/rp/parks.htm
Street Address: 301 West Main Street, Carrboro

Bathrooms: no
Stroller-friendly: yes
Food nearby: no—except during farmers' market
Picnic-friendly: yes
Recommended ages: 2-5 years old

Cost: free

Umstead Park

This large park has ample parking, basketball and tennis courts, softball field, picnic shelter, a large play structure, and plenty of swings. The sandy play area has a few bouncy spring-mounted rides. A fence prevents play from spilling over into Bolin Creek, but the trail leads over a bridge and into the woods along the creek, eventually leading uphill about half a mile to the Northside neighborhood, though toddlers generally prefer to loop back to the playground for just a taste of wilderness.

Hours: dawn to dusk

Contact Info:

Phone: (919) 968-2784 Chapel Hill Parks and Recreation Department
Website: www.townofchapelhill.org/index.asp?nid=68
Street address: 399 Umstead Drive, Chapel Hill

Bathrooms: no
Stroller-friendly: yes
Food nearby: no
Picnic-friendly: yes
Recommended ages: any, especially 5 to 9 year-olds

Cost: free

Wilson Park

Wilson Park has tennis courts, an athletic field, ample parking, and bathrooms open in warmer months. The playground has two play structures, one for toddlers and one for older children, with an impressively steep slide, set over mulch. The sand area has two sand diggers, so enthusiasts can dig together. There are plenty of swings, for both toddlers and bigger kids. Like the swings, the jungle gym has sand underneath and around it, providing for plenty of sand digging and building.

At the back of the park are two reservable picnic shelters, with tables and grills, and a path leading to the town's newly acquired Adams tract. This beautiful parcel of woods and trails connects to the path along Bolin Creek that ultimately leads to Chapel Hill High School. The paths are unpaved, bumpy, and steep in some places, but make for a pretty walk, especially on one of North Carolina's pretty winter days. Or walk downtown for a snack and ice cream!

Hours: dawn to dusk

Contact Info:
Phone: (919) 918-7364 Carrboro Recreation and Parks Department
Website: www.carrboro.com/parks.html, www.ci.carrboro.nc.us/rp/default.htm
Street address: 101 Williams Street, Carrboro

Bathrooms: yes, April through October
Stroller-friendly: yes
Food nearby: no, but downtown Carrboro is about half a mile away
Picnic-friendly: yes
Recommended ages: any

Cost: free

Efland-Cheeks Park

This park has plenty of space to play, with lighted basketball courts, athletic fields, walking track, and a playground with a new play structure and a cool swing apparatus. For gatherings or events, a meeting space, kitchen, and picnic shelters can be reserved in advance.

Hours: dawn to dusk

Contact Info:
Phone: (919) 563-1130
Website: www.co.orange.nc.us/recparks/efland-cheeks.asp
Street address: 117 Richmond Road, Mebane

Bathrooms: yes
Stroller-friendly: yes
Food nearby: no
Picnic-friendly: yes
Recommended ages: any

Cost: free

Exchange Club Park

Located on the original road into Hillsborough, the Exchange Park has two small playgrounds (one for older children and one for toddlers) with four swings and play structure, athletic fields, and a clubhouse. There is also creek nearby. The shelter may be reserved for group events. Traffic on the narrow road is quiet. Down the road, check out the original bridge, built in 1922 and recently refurbished, that spans over the railroad tracks beneath. A short walk away, downtown Hillsborough has restaurants and shops.

Hours: dawn to dusk

Contact Info:
Phone: (919) 732-9283
Street address: 331 Exchange Park Lane, Hillsborough

Bathrooms: yes
Stroller-friendly: yes
Food nearby: yes, in downtown Hillsborough
Picnic-friendly: yes
Recommended ages: any

Cost: free

Fairview Park

This park, special to Hillsborough's Fairview neighborhood, has natural areas with trails through trees and grass to an athletic field. The playground has a play structure good even for little ones, over a sand surface. Plans for basketball and tennis courts, more picnic space, improvements to the athletic field, and more trails are scheduled to be complete in 2009.

Hours: dawn to dusk

Contact Info:
Phone: (919) 245-2660 Orange County Recreation and Parks Department
Website: www.co.orange.nc.us/RecParks/fairview.asp
Street address: 501 Rainey Avenue, Hillsborough

Bathrooms: yes
Stroller-friendly: yes
Food nearby: no
Picnic-friendly: yes
Recommended ages: any

Cost: free

Lake Michael Park (see also Boating)

Find calm and beauty among the trees and wildlife of Mebane's 200 acre park. The walking trail, just .7 mile of "moderate difficulty," leads through pretty woods with views of the lake beyond. The playgrounds, "tot lots" with swings and tall, steep metal slides, sit within the shade of the trees, not far from the parking lot.

The park has a sand volleyball court as well as picnic shelters available for rent. The lake's boating opportunities include paddle boats and boat rides. Benches along the shore provide a welcome spot to look out over the water and watch a mysterious kind of water fowl preen its feathers.

Hours: mid-March, Monday, Thursday, Friday, Saturday 7am - 7pm, Sunday 1pm - 7pm; April through October, Monday, Thursday, Friday, Saturday 6am - dusk, Sunday 1pm - dusk. Closed November through mid-March.

Contact Info:
Phone: (919) 563-4573 or (919) 563-3629, ext. 8
Website: www.cityofmebane.com/lakemichaelpark.asp
Street Address: 7300 Lebanon Road, Mebane

Bathrooms: yes
Stroller-friendly: yes
Food nearby: no
Picnic-friendly: yes
Recommended ages: any

Cost: johnboat rental $4, fee to launch own boat $4, fishing $2 (license required), pontoon boat rides and paddle boat rental $1 per person, shelter fee $10. Children under 6, seniors 60 and over, and handicapped persons free.

Little River Park

On the Orange County line near Durham, this parcel of the Eno River has long trails, picnic tables, convenient parking, and of course plenty of nature. The plants and wildlife along the Eno River are diverse and interesting, though even a fish or the native shellfish can intrigue a child. The trails, quite steep in some places, are marked by green spots and numbered markers, and while the slightly shorter South River Trail wanders over three miles, a short cut allows hikers to loop back on the Ridge Trail, along the river. About eight miles of rather strenuous mountain bike trails have blue markers, and while hikers are permitted on these trails, the bicyclists have the right of way.

The playground is located near the picnic shelters, so you can watch children play while you prepare a picnic lunch. There's plenty of grass for running around, too. The picnic shelters may be reserved for gatherings or events. For campers there are tent pads and two fire rings. Group camping is available from February through mid-November.

Throughout the year, the Orange County Recreation and Parks Department holds classes and special programs for children. The toddler classes teach about nature through books, stories, and activities. Older children, or the whole family, can build birdhouses or plant trees or flowers. Pre-registration and a small fee are required.

Hours: daily, November - February 8am - 5pm, March and October 8am - 6pm, April and September 8am - 7pm. Closed Christmas Eve and Day and New Year's Day.

Contact Info:
Phone: (919) 732-5505 Little River Park office, (919) 245-2660 Orange County Recreation and Parks Department, (919) 732-5505 to register for classes.
Website: www.co.orange.nc.us/RecParks/little_river_park.asp , www.enoriver.org/eno/parks/LittleRiverPark.html
Street address: 301 Little River Park Way, off Guess Road, Durham

Bathrooms: yes (no showers)
Stroller-friendly: yes
Food nearby: no
Picnic-friendly: yes
Recommended ages: any

Cost: free; classes $5 or less

Pittsboro Kiwanis Playground

This playground has been thoughtfully designed, especially for very young children. All three play areas have a spongy plastic base, rather than sand or mulch, which dries quickly and provides a soft landing for vigorous playing. The play structure has slides and places to climb, without being too big for preschoolers. A squared-in space, perfect for little ones still crawling or just learning to stand, has handles and wheels to turn and twist and a low mirror for admiring oneself. A little playhouse at the back has musical devices, such as chimes and metal bowls, pleasing to hit and make sounds. A sidewalk with mosaic insets connects the three areas as well as a picnic table, bench, water fountain, and a stump with interesting possibilities. A green fence encloses the entire space, so even impetuous toddlers pelting across the grass will stay safe from the street.

Hours: dawn to dusk

Contact Info:
Street address: 309 Credle Street, Pittsboro

Bathrooms: no
Stroller-friendly: yes
Food nearby: no, but downtown Pittsboro is a short walk away
Picnic-friendly: yes
Recommended ages: any, especially 5 and under

Cost: free

Playgrounds at Jordan Lake

The playgrounds at the sites of Jordan Lake received new play structures, with cool slides and things to climb. The swings are nice, but don't have toddler seats. The playground sand provides satisfying digging, especially with all the pine needles and gumballs (from the sweet gum trees) available for decoration. Picnic tables are tucked into the shade nearby.

When the kids need a change from playing, the trails at most sites are neither very difficult or long. Pets are permitted, on leashes, but bicycles are not allowed. The 1.4 miles trail at Seaforth has interesting finds such as a hollow tree, bridges, and of course frogs and birds. Two trails at Ebenezer Church site, both less than a mile long, overlook the lake and loop around ponds. Bring extra clothes and shoes, for even if you do not intend to go swimming, even if it is one of those pretty February days when hiking is best, the mud and water near the lake's edge are too tempting and too interesting to resist.

Hours: November through February 8am - 6pm; March 8am - 7pm; April, September, and October 8am - 8pm, May through August 8am - 9pm. Closed Christmas Day.

Contact Info:
Phone: (919) 362-0586 park office
Website: www.ncparks.gov/Visit/parks/jord/main.php, ils.unc.edu/parkproject/visit/
For maps, of the whole lake or specific sites: ils.unc.edu/parkproject/visit/jord/jord.pdf

Street address: 280 State Park Road, Apex Park Office. Seaforth and Parker's Creek are off Highway 64; Ebenezer Church is on Beaver Creek Road, off Highway 64 East

Bathrooms: yes
Stroller-friendly: yes
Food nearby: no
Picnic-friendly: yes
Recommended ages: any

Cost: $5 per car, $3 for senior citizens 62 and up, $10 per bus, on weekends only during April, May, and September, and daily from Memorial Day to Labor Day. No charge from October through March. Annual passes available. Camping fees extra.

Hikes, Nature, and Animals

Adams Tract

This beautiful parcel of woods is named for the botany professor and his wife who bought the property in 1950, but the homestead was founded before the name of Carrboro itself. This park contains some impressively old trees; the trail leads past huge maples, through stands of pines and beech trees, and over some steep grades of hill, in a roughly 1.25-mile loop. At the foot of the hill, the Bolin Creek trail follows the creek (and the railroad tracks above) to Chapel Hill High School.

Despite the address, access to the trail starts at the back of Wilson Park on Williams Street. Parking here is safer, too, rather than along the narrow and busy Estes Drive Extension.

Hours: dawn to dusk

Contact Info:
Phone: (919) 918-7364 Carrboro Recreation and Parks Department
Website: www.ci.carrborro.nc.us/rp/default.html
Street Address: 207 Estes Drive Extenstion, Carrboro

Bathrooms: no
Stroller-friendly: no
Food nearby: no, but downtown Carrboro is a walkable half mile away
Picnic-friendly: yes
Recommended ages: any

Cost: free

Bolin Creek Trail

The paved greenway of Bolin Creek Trail begins at Chapel Hill's Community Center. Wide and mostly level, the trail intersects with neighborhoods, the library, and even a path to a coffee shop. The trail's evenness and lack of motorized traffic make it a good choice for strollers, bikes, or just quietly ambling through pretty creekland. The trail ends a mile and a half later at Martin Luther King Jr. Boulevard, conveniently near places to rest and refresh. For the more energetic and ambitious, another half mile walk across the street and down Umstead Road will bring you to Umstead Park and playground. Be careful, though, as this sidewalk is narrow.

Bolin Creek continues on, and while the greenway here does not yet exist, you can pick up the trail again in Carrboro, from Wilson Park. Wind down the marked paths of the beautiful Adams Tract to get to the creek again. Wide but rocky, and crossed occasionally by tiny streams, this unpaved easement along Bolin Creek is popular with joggers, families, and cyclists who dart up narrower paths to the impressive mountain bike extravaganza near Seawell School Road. Though all pets are required to be leashed, expect the occasional bounding large dog. From the main path, you'll find bridges leading to wooded tot lots, a long-abandoned Corvair, even the ruins of an old mill, and of course, the wildlife of the creek—fish, frogs, crayfish, native azaleas, and majestic blue heron. The trail ends at Chapel Hill High School, a longer distance than most small children can walk, so just take your time and turn around when you're ready.

Hours: dawn to dusk

Contact Info:
Phone: (919) 968-2784 Chapel Hill Parks and Recreation
Website: townhall.townofchapelhill.org/parks_&_rec/
Street address: 120 South Estes Drive, Chapel Hill

Bathrooms: no, except as found in nearby establishments
Stroller-friendly: yes
Food nearby: no
Picnic-friendly: no
Recommended ages: any

Cost: free

Duke Forest

Duke Forest consists of over 7,000 acres of woods, creeks, and trails, preserved and carefully managed by Duke University. You can access different parcels in Durham, Orange, and Alamance Counties. In some places, you may see signs explaining forestry methods or describing the types of trees, for Duke Forest is the site of many educational programs. For the rest of us, it's a beautiful place to wander. In addition to many kinds of animals and plants, the forest holds the remnants of old homeplaces and mills.

Two of the most popular access points lie off Erwin Road near Pickett Road, and off Whitfield Road near the New Hope Fire Station Drive in Durham. Be careful when parking along these fast roads! The unpaved trails lead through stands of hardwoods and pines, up hills, and down to New Hope Creek, where you're sure to find a lovely rock or spot for a picnic. Though camping is not permitted, the public is welcome to go run, bike, ride horses, walk their dogs (on leashes), or simply enjoy the outdoors. You can, for $7, buy a detailed map of Duke Forest and its trails at Duke University's bookstore, send $8 to Office of the Duke Forest, Box 90332, Durham, NC 27708-0332, or order from the website. The website's downloadable map works fine for most purposes, though.

Hours: dawn to dusk

Contact Info:
Phone: (919) 613-8013
Website: www.dukeforest.duke.edu
Street address: varies— Whitfield Road, Erwin Road near Pickett Road are two well-known access points, with some room to park along the road.

Bathrooms: no
Stroller-friendly: no
Food nearby: no
Picnic-friendly: yes
Recommended ages: any

Cost: free

Fearrington Village Trails

Fine gravel trails wind in and around Fearrington Village's neighborhoods and gardens and up to the Village Market, with restaurants, shops, and an excellent book store. While smooth enough for bikes, the trail carries quite a bit of foot traffic, so be careful of people out walking. Unlike nature trails, these walks have no threat of poison ivy or snakes—just a few drowsy cows, and the occasional brisk pedestrian.

Hours: dawn to dusk

Contact Info:
Phone: (919) 542-4000
Website: www.fearrington.com/living/parks.asp
Street address: 2000 Fearrington Village Center, Pittsboro

Bathrooms: no
Stroller-friendly: yes (if your stroller can handle gravel)
Food nearby: yes
Picnic-friendly: yes
Recommended ages: any

Cost: free

Little River Park Trails

The Little River Park has seven miles of hiking trails, each marked with numbers, symbols, and signs. The South River Trail is the shorter of the three trails at roughly three miles. The terrain is challenging in places, but offers many beautiful views and natural areas.

Hours: daily, May through September 7am - dusk, October through April 8am - dusk. Closed Christmas Eve, Christmas Day, and New Year's Day.

Contact Info:
Phone: (919) 732-5505 River Park office, (919)245-2660 Orange County Recreation and Parks Department.
Website: www.enoriver.org/eno/parks/LittleRiverPark.html, www.co.orange.nc.us/RecParks/little_river_park.asp
Street address: 301 Little River Park Way, off Guess Road, Durham

Bathrooms: yes
Stroller-friendly: no
Food nearby: no
Picnic-friendly: yes
Recommended ages: any

Cost: free

Occaneechee Mountain Park

Now that it's part of Eno River State Park, the trails and parking on Occoneechee Mountain have improved quite a bit. There's a bathroom right at the parking area, and maps at the trail head show long and short routes around the mountain. The wide gravel road, though steep, leads to a beautiful outcropping of rocks and a glorious view from the top of the cliff—trees and blue sky reflected in the calm waters of the Eno River. When the new observation deck is complete, the view should be even more spectacular.

Descending down the other side involves a *lot* of stairs. Looking back up at the pink and silvery cliff from below is almost as breathtaking as the view from above. The path continues down more stairs, toward the river, where the mountain laurels and wildlife resemble those of the North Carolina mountains. Springs and rocks add to the enchantment of this place. Beside the river at last, children can throw sticks and rocks into the water or watch and listen for birds. Some species of birds here can't be found anywhere else this far east of the mountains. The climb back to the parking lot takes time, and while children five or six and older will manage fine, preschoolers and toddlers may need a lift, so plan accordingly and perhaps bring a backpack or carrier.

Hours: dawn to dusk

Contact Info:
Phone: (919) 383-1686 Eno River State Park office
Website: www.enoriver.org/eno/parks/Occoneechee.htm, ncparks.gov/Visit/parks/ocmo/main.php
Street address: Virginia Cates Road, off Orange Grove Road, Hillsborough

Bathrooms: yes
Stroller-friendly: no
Food nearby: no
Picnic-friendly: yes
Recommended ages: any

Cost: free

Poet's Walk at Ayr Mount

The Poet's Walk is a lovely, one-mile path around the woods and gracious lawns of Hillsborough's historic Ayr Mount estate. The trail leads past willow trees, picnic tables, and a place to pick up cards and pencils to compose a poem. It continues to loop around, through the woods, down to the Eno River, up past an ancient Native American trading path, and back to the house. The beautiful surroundings can be distracting, so watch your step for tree roots and stay on the path to avoid poison ivy. Numerous benches, with such names as "Footbridge Rest," provide places to stop and contemplate a view or greet people walking their leashed dogs. At Reflection Pond Rest you may also discover paper cups and a cooler of water. With stops and drinks, the walk takes roughly thirty minutes, gentle enough for a preschooler.

The wide grassy lawns are perfect for a game of chase or tossing a ball. Rest in the adirondack chairs on the stone patio and take in the view. Tours of the house, a rare brick federal-style house dating back to 1815, may interest older children.

Hours: daily, November through January 9am - 5pm, March, April, September, October 9am - 6pm, May and August 9am - 7pm, June and July 9am - 8pm.

Contact Info:
Phone: (919) 732-6886
Website: www.classicalamericanhomes.org
Street address: 376 St. Mary's Road, Hillsborough

Bathrooms: no
Stroller-friendly: no
Food nearby: no
Picnic-friendly: yes
Recommended ages: preschoolers and up

Cost: free; house tours $10 per person March 21 through December 20

Talking Trees Trail at Jordan Lake Educational State Forest

The Education Center at Jordan Lake has outdoor exhibits, ranger-led classes, and picnic facilities for enjoying this natural area. The Talking Tree Trail has an informational recording at each of seven trees along the three-quarter mile loop. The Forest Demonstration Trail, at 1.5 miles, is longer but not strenuous. The park ranger talks, designed to complement the North Carolina education curriculum, are free but require pre-registration.

Hours: mid-March to mid-November, Tuesday through Friday 9am - 5pm, Saturday and Sunday 11am - 8pm. Closes at 5pm on weekends December to mid-March. Closed Thanksgiving and Christmas.

Contact Info:
Phone: (919) 542-1154
Website: www.ncesf.org/JLESF/home.htm, ncparks.gov/Visit/parks/jord/activities.php
Street address: 2632 Big Woods Road, Chapel Hill (Chatham County)

Bathrooms: yes
Stroller-friendly: yes
Food nearby: no
Picnic-friendly: yes
Recommended ages: any, but especially grades K-6

Cost: free with pre-registration

Town Lake Park

Occupying the land behind Pittsboro Elementary School, Town Lake Park was originally known as Jaycees Park before the Jaycees turned the park over to the town. While the playground and athletics fields are scheduled for much-needed renovation, the walking trail even now is just right for children. Comprised of dirt and wooden walkways, and a bridge, the trail encircles the 38 acre lake formed from Robeson Creek, a feeder creek for the Haw River. With improvements, this park will provide a lovely destination within walking distance of downtown Pittsboro.

Hours: dawn to dusk

Contact Info:

Street Address: Lake Drive, off Goldston Road/ Highway 87, Pittsboro

Bathrooms: no
Stroller-friendly: no
Food nearby: no
Picnic-friendly: yes
Recommended ages: any

Cost: free

UNC Campus

The UNC campus offers places to walk and play, as long as you go when students aren't changing classes. The brick sidewalks are fun for riding bikes or scooters, and the grassy quads have squirrels to chase, tree roots to step on, and room for a game of chase. McCorkle Place, situated on Franklin Street across from the downtown, has such intriguing monuments as the cement-filled Davie Poplar and the Old Well. From here you can reach several kid-friendly restaurants, the Ackland Art Museum, the Planetarium, and the Coker Arboretum.

Across Cameron Avenue and past South Building lies Polk Place, with more criss-crossing sidewalks, interesting bumps and ramps, and Wilson Library to the south. Inside Wilson Library, the North Carolina Collection Gallery has many historical exhibits and completely restored historical rooms. Past exhibits have included antique postcards and Sir Walter Raleigh. History-minded children, especially fourth graders studying the state, may enjoy a stop here.

The UNC Student Stores have the excellent Bulls Head Bookstore and UNC attire and souvenirs. Manning Hall has children's books that the public can check out with a campus library card, available at Davis Library. The picture book collection in the main lobby is superlative, and it's just the tip of the iceberg. The stacks contain far more children's books. However, as the Library Science graduate school library, this not a place for kids to romp or have story time; people will be studying.

If your walk stretches into Friday evening, catch some music and food at the Carolina Inn, or find dinner at one of the many downtown restaurants.

UNC Campus:
Hours: any time

NC Collection Gallery:
Hours: Monday through Friday 9am - 5pm, Saturday 9am - 1pm, Sunday 1pm - 5pm. Closed on state holidays.

Contact Info:(UNC Campus)
Website: www.unc.edu/visitors
Street address: South Building, Cameron Avenue, Chapel Hill

Contact Info: (NC Collection)
Phone: (919) 962-1172
Website: www.lib.unc.edu/ncc/gallery.html
Street address: UNC Campus, Raleigh Road, Chapel Hill

Bathrooms: yes
Stroller-friendly: yes
Food nearby: yes
Picnic-friendly: yes
Recommended ages: any

Cost: free

White Pines Nature Preserve

This 275 acre oasis of pine trees was the first tract acquired by the Triangle Land Conservancy. The trails are at least a mile long and, in places, steeply downhill, offering beautiful views of both the Deep and Rocky Rivers, and leading through this rare stand of tree species not found anywhere else east of the Blue Ridge Mountains. The trails overall are rated as moderately difficult. A map of the trails is available at the Triangle Land Conservancy website.

Hours: dawn to dusk

Contact Info:
Phone: (919) 833-3662 Triangle Land Conservancy
Website: www.tlc-nc.org/lands/tlc/white_pines_np.shtml
Street address: South Rocky River Road, Pittsboro

Bathrooms: no
Stroller-friendly: no
Food nearby: no
Picnic-friendly: yes
Recommended ages: school-aged and up

Cost: free

FARMS AND NATURE

Carrboro Farmers' Market

Twice a week at the Town Commons, you'll find flowers, plants, organic produce and meat, hand-made soaps, fresh baked goods, and arts and crafts, all produced within fifty miles of Carrboro. Many of the vendors return year after year, and developing a relationship with the farmers and the food is one of the unexpected benefits of shopping here. The hubbub of the crowd on Saturday mornings is part of the fun, as the scene is as social as it is commercial. Wednesday afternoons are less crowded, though sometimes with less selection. Bringing your own bags and plenty of change will make transactions easier. Parking at the farmers' market is limited, but street parking is available within a short walk.

The Market holds a few events during the year, such as cooking demonstrations and the Tomato Tasting, and has expanded to Southern Village, where it opens on Thursday afternoons, on the Village Lawn.

Hours: Saturday 7am - 12pm year-round, Wednesday 3:30 - 6:30 April through December. Southern Village, Thursday 4pm - 7pm May through December.

Contact Info:
Website: www.carrborofarmersmarket.com
Street address: 301 West Main Street, Carrboro, or the Village Lawn, Market Street, Chapel Hill

Bathrooms: no
Stroller-friendly: yes, though it can be crowded
Food nearby: yes
Picnic-friendly: yes, especially at nearby town hall lawn
Recommended ages: all

Cost: varies by product, free for the experience

CFSA Piedmont Farm Tour

The Carolina Farm Stewardship Association sponsors this tour of local farms, dairies, and vineyards to support sustainable farming in North Carolina. The Farm Tour map includes not only locations of participating farms, but also descriptions of the farms and suggestions for the most kid-friendly sites. The ticket (a button) is good for both days, and because you choose the farms you want to visit, you can go at your own pace. Expect to visit at most four farms per day. The people at the farms often have delicious produce and goods for sale. The farm tourists tend to be a knowledgeable, friendly bunch, so while parking at some places can be challenging, the mood overall is easy-going. The Piedmont Farm Tour is a real highlight for our family, seeing the harmony these farmers have built with their land and animals, and enjoying the farm settings in springtime.

Hours: last weekend in April, Saturday and Sunday 1pm - 5pm

Contact Info:
Phone: (919) 542-2402
Website: www.carolinafarmstewards.org
Street address: varies

Bathrooms: at some farms; at farms with animals, foot-operated wash stations available
Stroller-friendly: varies; backpack or carrier might work better, due to rough terrain or crowds
Food nearby: yes
Picnic-friendly: yes
Recommended ages: any

Cost: $30 per car for all farms at the first farm you visit, $25 advance tickets available at many local businesses, or $10 per car per farm.

Haw River Assembly and Festival (see also Festivals)

The Haw River Assembly works year-round to protect the river's water, lands, and wildlife. For three weeks in the spring or fall, performers and educators host learning labs for fourth graders on the river itself. They study such topics as water monitoring and the cultural history associated with the river. These labs culminate in the Haw River Festival, with booths and presentations about the river's history and the Assembly's on-going efforts to improve and preserve water quality.

The Assembly also offers information about hiking and boating on the Haw River, including paddling clubs and local outfitters that offer a variety of options and services for exploring the river firsthand, as well as up-to-date information about known hazards and flow statistics. Despite its generally serene appearance, the Haw can be quite dangerous when the water level and currents run high, as after a heavy rain. Check the Assembly's website for more boating information.

Hours: Festival, second Saturday in May, 1pm - 6pm. For other events, check website or call.

Contact Info:
Phone: (919) 542-5790
Website: www.hawriver.org
Street address: old Bynum bridge, foot of Bynum Road, Bynum

Bathrooms: yes
Stroller-friendly: yes
Food nearby: yes
Picnic-friendly: yes
Recommended ages: any

Cost: for festival, adults $5, children under 14 $3, babies free

North Carolina Botanical Gardens

Walking on the trails of the Botanical Gardens is a great family activity any time of year. Even though the Gardens' address says Laurel Hill Road, take Mason Farm Road to the parking lot. Eventually, this will be the site of the new "green" Visitor Education Center, under construction since late 2007. Behind the parking lot, the Piedmont Nature Trails lead up hills and over creeks through peaceful woods. This is a hike even a preschooler enjoys. The fall and winter seasons are especially pleasant times to take a nature walk without the bother of bugs or undergrowth.

Across Laurel Hill Road are the gates to the gardens and Totten Center. The fairy garden and giant chess board are especially appealing, as is the patio with large planters and numerous paths lined with labels, art, and some funny surprises. The Totten Center itself has a library, art exhibits, and small gift shop. Self-guides, summer camps, and programs for schools or other groups all emphasize hands-on exploration and use of the senses. For upper elementary grades, these classes also examine the cultural aspect of nature and horticulture. Each class lasts about an hour and costs $30 for groups of thirty students or fewer. For families, there are special events such as weekly story times beginning in April and continuing during the warmer months. Discovering Magic in the Garden, held each May, invites families to wear magical costumes and hear stories, make crafts, and listen to music. Bring your wings!

Hours: Monday through Friday 8am - 5pm; Saturday 9am - 5pm; Sunday 1pm - 5pm.

Closes at 6pm on weekends during Daylight Saving Time (March to November).

Contact Info:
Phone: (919) 962-0522
Website: www.ncbg.unc.edu
Street Address: 1000 Laurel Hill Road, Chapel Hill

Bathrooms: yes
Stroller-friendly: yes, though backpack might work better on trails
Food nearby: no
Picnic-friendly: yes
Recommended ages: any

Cost: free

Spence's Farm

This laid-back farm has lots of horses and other farm animals, gardens, and many after-school and summer programs. The farm sells the eggs from their chickens (or the chickens themselves), and the barn has a tall hay bale maze, a popular activity for birthday parties. In October, they hold their annual Halloween Harvest Festival, and twice a year they host horseback riding exhibitions. Their indoor riding arena, a relatively new addition to the farm, provides protected space not only for riding horses but also for classes and parties. Enrichment classes throughout the year teach skills such as horsemanship, woodworking, art, metalworking, and pottery. The atmosphere at Spence's farm is positive, and the trained staff seek to encourage students' personal knowledge and respect for each other and for nature.

Hours: varies by program

Contact Info:
Phone: (919) 968-8581
Website: www.spencesfarm.com
Street address: 6407 Mill House Road, Chapel Hill

Bathrooms: yes
Stroller-friendly: yes
Food nearby: no
Picnic-friendly: yes
Recommended ages: any

Cost: varies

The Rocks Gemstone Mining and Trading Post

The first thing you might notice when you pull into the driveway of The Rocks is the long, water-free sluice. You can pan for gems or even gold here, at your own pace. A mere six dollars will buy you a bag of sand guaranteed to contain amethysts, quartz, emerald, or jade. They have rocks from all over the world here, and geodes, as well as metal detectors, deer feeders, and jewelry. There's even a playground with a playhouse for little ones and a picnic area. This is the destination of choice for those who love rocks, crystals, and gems.

Hours: Tuesday through Saturday 10am - 5pm (closed for lunch from 12:30pm - 1:30pm)

Closed Sunday. Monday by appointment only.

Contact Info:
Phone: (919) 542-6112
Website: www.ncgems.com
Street address: 17 Gem Mine Drive, Moncure/ 535-A Old Sanford Road, Moncure

Bathrooms: yes
Stroller-friendly: yes
Food nearby: no
Picnic-friendly: yes
Recommended ages: any, but especially 4 and up

Cost: varies by bag type, $6 and up. Group discounts available.

ANIMALS

Carnivore Preservation Trust

A refuge for tigers, ocelots, leopards and other cats, CPT has a mission to preserve and rescue various endangered species of carnivores. The guided tours, lasting at least an hour and a half, take you very near the animals and teach about each species, the history of the Trust, and the stories of the animals themselves. The CPT might be a good outing for children who love animals, though the animals' histories are often sad, and adults must sign a waiver for children under 18 years of age. Birthday packages are available. The Paws and Shop gift shop has T-shirts, bookmarks, tote bags, and magnets. While not inexpensive, the CPT performs an important service, and all proceeds go to caring for these beautiful and endangered animals.

Hours: by reservation only, Saturday and Sunday 10am and 1pm

Contact Info:
Phone: (919) 542-4684
Website: www.cptigers.org
Street address: 1940 Hanks Chapel Road, Pittsboro

Bathrooms: yes
Stroller-friendly: yes
Food nearby: no
Picnic-friendly: yes
Recommended ages: any

Cost: adults $12/ $10 January to March; Children 4-14 $7/$5 Jan. to March; children 3 and under free.

Celebrity Dairy

This goat farm uses sustainable farming practices and local markets to create its award-winning chevre cheeses. The farm is a popular field trip destination, and the dairy's Inn is an acclaimed bed and breakfast.

Twice a year, the dairy opens to the public on "Open Barn" days. In February, on the weekend before Valentine's Day, people can come and see the baby goats. Due to state regulations, visitors can no longer hold the baby goats, but you can still see and pet them, feed the older kids, and enjoy the beauty of the farm. Dress for the weather—when it's cold out, it's even cooler in the barn. Though crowded, the event is casual and low-key. You can bring a picnic or buy drinks and food, most notably two kinds of delicious homemade soup, from the Inn. Foot-operated handwashing stations around the farm remind visitors to clean their hands.

The rest of the year, people may come to view the goats at milking time, 6am and 6pm daily. In April, the dairy is a favorite stop on the Piedmont Farm Tour. In November, the dairy holds the second Open Barn, the Sunday after Thanksgiving. People can tour the barn, see the goats (older now), swing on the rope swing, eat, and visit with each other at this unique and friendly farm.

Hours: Open Barn: February, Saturday and Sunday before Valentine's Day, 12pm - 5pm; November, Sunday after Thanksgiving, 1pm - 5pm. Daily milkings: 6am and 6pm.

Contact Info:
Phone: (919) 742-5176
Website: www.celebritydairy.com
Street address: 144 Celebrity Dairy Way, Siler City/ 2106 Mt Vernon Hickory Mountain Road, Siler City

Bathrooms: yes
Stroller-friendly: yes, though a backpack might work better in the crowds
Food nearby: yes
Picnic-friendly: yes
Recommended ages: any

Cost: free

Fearrington Village's Belted Galloways and Fainting Goats

On a pretty day, a visit to the gentle animals at Fearrington Village makes a nice outing, especially for the younger children. The Belted Galloway cows, a Scottish breed of beef cattle, have a picturesque stripe of white in their otherwise black fur. Sometimes a calf can be seen huddling close to its mother. Several of the cows have won awards at the State Fair, but success hasn't gone to their heads. They're the same curious, kindly creatures they ever were.

When frightened, the Belted Tennessee Fainting Goats may appear to faint. If only a little startled, they might just freeze, but if really scared, they fall over as if stiff and dead. But they're really ok. The donkeys with them protect the cattle and will chase away or attack any canine predators. The whirligigs by Vallis Simpson of Wilson and the silo nearby make a charming backdrop for the animals, so take a leisurely stroll around the pasture and village square. You can take pictures or buy souvenirs of the animals at The Belted Goat.

Hours: any time

Contact Info:
Phone: (919) 542-2121 Fearrington Village; (919) 542-1145 The Belted Goat shop
Website: www.fearrington.com/village/cows.asp
Street address: Village Way, Pittsboro, NC

Bathrooms: yes
Stroller-friendly: yes
Food nearby: yes
Picnic-friendly: yes
Recommended ages: any

Cost: free

Jordan Lake Ranger Talks

Did you know Jordan Lake rangers offer educational programs for groups? All you have to do is fill out and submit a form (available online) at least two weeks in advance. Rangers will schedule talks Tuesday through Sunday as early as 9:30 in the morning.

Several talks teach about animals that live at the lake, such as bald eagles, beavers, birds of prey, reptiles and amphibians, and fish. Other talks focus on experiencing nature, such as recognizing animal tracks and signs, hiking skills (for children ages eight and up), night sounds, and a very popular fishing class for children ages six to twelve.

Rangers also lead nature hikes or assist in the Be a Junior Ranger program, in which kids complete activities delineated in a pamphlet from the park office, though any adult supervision will suffice.

Hours: Tuesday through Sunday, 9:30am or later, by appointment

Contact Info:
Phone: (919) 362-0586
Website: www.ncparks.gov/Visit/parks/jord/activities.php
For talk descriptions and form: www.ils.unc.edu/parkproject/visit/jord/i&e.pdf
Street Address: 280 State Park Road, Apex

Bathrooms: yes
Stroller-friendly: varies
Food nearby: no
Picnic-friendly: yes
Recommended ages: K+

Cost: entrance fees only ($5 per car, $10 per bus, Memorial Day through Labor Day, and weekends in April, May, and September, or $40/summer pass)

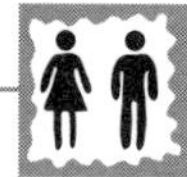

Woof-A-Palooza

Held by Chatham Animal Rescue and Education, this fundraiser begins with a one-mile walk with a canine friend. After the walk, there are demonstrations, entertainment, and contests—with prizes—such as owner-pet look-alike. Vendors sell food and pet supplies and accessories. With fun for a good cause, this event raises money for the care of rescued animals with special needs, and in what better company than happy dogs?

Hours: mid-September, 10am - 2pm

Contact Info:
Phone: (919) 542-5757 Chatham Animal Rescue and Education
Website: www.chathamanimalrescue.org
Street address: 764 West Street, Pittsboro (Central Carolina Community College)

Bathrooms: yes
Stroller-friendly: yes
Food nearby: yes
Picnic-friendly: yes
Recommended ages: any

Cost: $25 registration per dog, plus any donations

RECREATION AND SPORTS

SWIMMING

A. D. Clark Pool

During the summer, this pool comes alive with kids and families. Located behind the Hargraves Center, the fenced-in outdoor pool has a baby pool beside it. Locker rooms and family changing area have recently been renovated. Swimming lessons are available during the summer through the Chapel Hill Parks and Recreation Department.

Hours: Memorial Day through Labor Day

Contact Info:
Phone: (919) 968-2794
Website: townhall.townofchapelhill.org/parks_&_rec/facilities_greenways_&_parks/facilities/aquatics/
Street address: 216 North Roberson Street, Chapel Hill

Bathrooms: yes
Stroller-friendly: yes
Food nearby: no
Picnic-friendly: yes
Recommended ages: any

Cost: varies

Chapel Hill Community Center Pool

The newly renovated pool Chapel Hill Community Center Indoor Pool has a number of improvements including new roof and windows, zero-depth entry, and improved lockers and showers, with family changing areas. The schedule has three lap swim times during the week, and open swim times on the weekends and after school in the afternoons, as well as classes and swim team practice. Swimming lessons are affordable and well-taught. The pool schedule changes, so call or check the website.

Hours: Monday through Friday 5:30am - 8:30pm, Saturday 9am - 7:30pm, Sunday 12:30pm - 7:30pm

Contact Info:
Phone: (919) 968-2790
Website: townhall.townofchapelhill.org/parks_&_rec/facilities_greenways_&_parks/facilities/aquatics
Street address: 120 South Estes Drive, Chapel Hill

Bathrooms: yes
Stroller-friendly: yes
Food nearby: vending machines only
Picnic-friendly: yes (outside)
Recommended ages: varies

Cost: children 5 years and younger $1 resident, $2 non-resident; children 6-18 $2 resident, $4 non-resident, adults $3 resident, $6 non-resident. Twenty-visit, monthly, and annual passes available for residents and non-residents.

Homestead Aquatic Center

The newest swimming facility in Chapel Hill, the Aquatic Center has a large lap pool just for competitions and lap swimmers. The smaller, shallower pool, with warm water and zero-depth entry, is for classes and recreational swimmers. The building has bleachers, locker rooms, offices, and a reception room, as well as glass mosaic art by artist Ray King.

Hours: varies, so check website or call

Contact Info:
Phone: (919) 968-2784 Chapel Hill Parks and Recreation Department
Website: townhall.townofchapelhill.org/parks_&_rec/facilities_greenways_&_parks/facilities/aquatics/
Street Address: 300 Northern Park Drive, Chapel Hill

Bathrooms: yes
Stroller-friendly: yes
Food nearby: no
Picnic-friendly: at nearby park
Recommended ages: any

Cost: varies

Jordan Lake (see also Parks and Playgrounds)

There are four public swimming areas at Jordan Lake. Seaforth and Ebenezer Church have sandy beaches for digging or sunbathing, and a roped off swimming area. Parker Creek, in quiet section of the lake, has no motor boat traffic to disturb the water. Picnic tables and restrooms with showers and changing rooms are close by. Poplar Point has a sandy beach as well, and many campsites, but the restrooms are across the parking lot.

A limited number of life jackets hang prominently near the beach, but you may want to bring your own. The beaches at Jordan Lake have *no* lifeguards.

Hours: November through February 8am - 6pm; March 8am - 7pm; April, September, and October 8am - 8pm, May through August 8am - 9pm. Closed Christmas Day.

Contact Info:
Phone: (919) 362-0586 Park Office
Website: www.ncparks.gov/Visit/parks/jord/main.php, ils.unc.edu/parkproject/visit/
for maps, of the whole lake or specific sites: ils.unc.edu/parkproject/visit/jord/jord.pdf

Street address: 280 State Park Road, Apex Park Office. Seaforth and Parker's Creek are off Highway 64; Ebenezer Church is on Beaver Creek Road, off Highway 64 East.

Bathrooms: yes
Stroller-friendly: yes
Food nearby: no
Picnic-friendly: yes
Recommended ages: any

Cost: $5 per car, $3 for senior citizens 62 and up, $10 per bus, on weekends only during April, May, and September, and daily from Memorial Day to Labor Day. No charge from October through March. Annual passes available. Camping fees extra.

Meadowmont Swim Club

Meadowmont Swim Club is the area's only private pool open to the public with daily passes. The main pool is well-designed for fun for swimmers of all strengths. The shallow end has a graduated entry, with a gentle slope instead of steps, so even toddlers can wade or sit more safely. They will likely want to play in the shower of water from the big, red umbrella-like structure. Adults are welcome to bring a short deck chair into the water with them to stay close to their children. The big water slide is fun for older kids (and their adults), and well separated from the shallow end. The lifeguards are known to be serious, attentive, and safety-minded.

Unlike at some other pools, there's no mandated regular break, so if you're going for the day, you can swim as long as you want. When swimmers need a change of activity, a playground stands nearby, as well as a volleyball court and a basketball goal. A second pool offers lanes for lap swimming. The food is good—handmade sandwiches, pizza, and ice cream—but the line moves slowly, so get in line early or pack your own lunch (limited to one small cooler). The seating area at the shallow end is shaded only by perforated awnings, so plan ahead with hats and sunscreen, especially for the fair-skinned.

Summer camps, swimming lessons, and reservations for parties and events are available. Check the calendar for events throughout the year. This pool is a real treat for a special day out in the sun.

Hours: June to August 24, daily 10am - 9pm. August 25 to September, weekdays 1pm - 8pm and weekends 10am - 8pm. September weekdays 1pm - 7pm and weekends 10am - 7pm. Labor Day 10am - 8pm.

Contact Info:
Phone: (919) 945-0640
Website: www.meadowmontclub.com
Street address: 301 Old Barn Lane, Chapel Hill

Bathrooms: yes
Stroller-friendly: yes
Food nearby: yes
Picnic-friendly: yes (one cooler limit)
Recommended ages: any

Cost: adults $9 weekdays, $12 weekends; children 3-10 $9 weekdays, $10 weekends; children 0-2 free. Memorial Day, July 4th, Labor Day $15 per person. 10-visit pass $85.

Triangle Sportsplex (see also Gyms)

The Sportsplex has three pools: a six-foot deep lap pool, a baby pool, and a shallow recreation pool with a ramp for safer entry. It offers swim meets, swimming lessons, and after school and summer camp programs. The Sportsplex Grill serves sandwiches, snacks, salads, and other food and drinks. On summer mornings, the pool becomes lively with a good-natured and friendly crowd of campers, making swimming fun, if a bit loud.

Hours: Monday through Saturday 5:30am - 10pm, Sunday 12pm - 7pm

Contact Info:
Phone: (919) 644-0339
Website: www.trianglesportsplex.com
Street address: 1 Dan Kidd Drive, Hillsborough

Bathrooms: yes
Stroller-friendly: yes
Food nearby: yes
Picnic-friendly: no
Recommended ages: any

Cost: varies, according to activity

BOATING

Cane Creek Reservoir

About eight miles west of Carrboro on highway 54, on the right, stand the gates of Cane Creek Reservoir, which opened in 1993 as the larger of OWASA's two main municipal water supplies. Cane Creek Reservoir covers over five hundred acres, with open grassy areas and a wide lake. Stocked with at least four different kinds of fish, this lake reportedly offers excellent fishing, especially in the spring. Flat-bottomed johnboats and canoes are available for rent, and some private boats are permitted on the lake. To protect the water quality and wildlife, the staff must inspect that all boats are clean and use electric motors only. Boats on trailers are not allowed Electric motors are available for rent as well, but keep in mind the lake is large. There are no lifeguards or swimming here. If you do not have your own life preservers, you may borrow life jackets for adults and children. In past years, OWASA has opened both the Reservoir and University Lake free to customers bearing a bill or other proof of residence on "Free Fridays" in July and August. Bring a picnic and spend an afternoon away from town.

Hours: March through mid-November, Thursday through Saturday 6:30am - 6pm, Sunday 1pm - 6pm. Closed on the Friday before Easter, but open Memorial Day, July 4th and Labor Day.

Contact Info:
Phone: (919) 942-5790
Website: www.owasa.org/pages/canecreek.asp
Street address: 8705 Stanford Road, Chapel Hill

Bathrooms: yes
Stroller-friendly: yes
Food nearby: no
Picnic-friendly: yes
Recommended ages: any

Cost: boat rental: For OWASA customers and Orange County residents: adults $7.00, $3 for each additional adult; children 12 and under and seniors 65 and over $1.25. Electric trolling motor rentals: additional $13.50. (Boats, canoes and electric motors are rented by the half-day.) Discount season passes available.

Non-Orange County residents: $11.50 for the first person and $4.50 for each additional adult. Children and seniors: $1.25. Electric trolling motors: $19.00.

Jordan Lake (see also Parks and Playgrounds)

From the shore, the sight of sailboats on the blue water is one of the prettiest this lake affords. From a boat, you can enjoy the view of 150 miles of protected coastline and wildlife such as summering bald eagles, not to mention some good fishing. The lake's size gives waterskiers and motorboats a good ride. Vista Point reportedly has excellent winds for sailing. All sites have some kind of launch area, and Crosswinds has a private marina which rents pontoons and fishing boats for the day, half-day, or two hours or more. Ebenezer Church and Robeson Creek ramps are open twenty-four hours.

If you like to combine camping with your boating, family campsites at Poplar Point and Crosswinds also have access to beaches and swimming. Backpack camping is available at the New Hope site, and groups can camp at either Vista Point or Parkers Creek.

Hours: daily, November through February 8am - 6pm; March 8am - 7pm; April, September, and October 8am - 8pm, May through August 8am - 9pm. Closed Christmas Day.

Contact Info:
Phone: (919) 362-0586 Park Office
Website: www.ncparks.gov/Visit/parks/jord/main.php, ils.unc.edu/parkproject/visit/ for maps, of the whole lake or specific sites: ils.unc.edu/parkproject/visit/jord/jord.pdf

Street address: 280 State Park Road, Apex Park Office. Seaforth and Parker's Creek are off Highway 64; Ebenezer Church is on Beaver Creek Road, off Highway 64 East.

Bathrooms: yes
Stroller-friendly: yes
Food nearby: no
Picnic-friendly: yes
Recommended ages: any

Cost: $5 per car, $3 for senior citizens 62 and up, $10 per bus, on weekends only during April, May, and September, and daily from Memorial Day to Labor Day. No charge from October through March. Annual passes available. Camping fees extra.

Lake Michael (see also Parks and Playgrounds)

Enjoy the outdoors from a boat on this 59 acre lake. Paddle boat rental and pontoon boat rides are very reasonably priced. You can rent a johnboat, or bring your own boat, and enjoy the excellent fishing opportunities for bass, catfish, bream and other common fish on this quiet and pretty tree-lined lake.

Hours: mid-March, Monday, Thursday, Friday, Saturday 7am - 7pm, Sunday 1pm - 7pm. April through October, Monday, Thursday, Friday, Saturday 6am - dusk, Sunday 1pm - dusk. Closed November through mid-March.

Contact Info:
Phone: (919) 563-4573 or (919) 563-3629, ext. 8
Website: www.cityofmebane.com/lakemichaelpark.asp
Street Address: 7300 Lebanon Road, Mebane

Bathrooms: yes
Stroller-friendly: yes
Food nearby: no
Picnic-friendly: yes
Recommended ages: any

Cost: johnboat rental $4, fee to launch own boat $4, fishing $2 (license required), pontoon boat rides and paddle boat rental $1 per person, shelter fee $10. Children under 6, seniors 60 and over, and handicapped persons free.

University Lake

This pretty, 213 acre lake has picnic areas, excellent fishing, and boating opportunities. You can rent canoes or johnboats—or bring your own scull, kayak, or any boat you can bring on your car *without* a trailer. Electric motors only are allowed on the lake, which supplies water to Chapel Hill and Carrboro, and lake staff will inspect any boat for cleanliness. The woods and creeks surrounding this lake have turtles, blue heron, and several kinds of stocked fish. Traditionally, in July and August, OWASA has held "Free Fridays," when residents and OWASA customers, with their latest water bill or identification in hand, can recreate at the lake, or Cane Creek Reservoir, for free. Life preservers are available for adults and children, or bring your own.

Hours:
March to November, Friday through Monday, 6:30am - 6pm

Contact Info:
Phone: (919) 942-8007
Website: www.owasa.org/pages/unlake.asp, www.carrboro.com/universitylake.html
Street address: South Old Fayetteville Road, Carrboro

Bathrooms: yes
Stroller-friendly: yes
Food nearby: vending machines
Picnic-friendly: yes
Recommended ages: any

Cost: half-day rentals. Boats: OWASA customers and Orange County residents, $6 for the first person and $2.50 each additional adult; children under 12 and seniors 65 and over, $1. Electric trolling motor: additional $12.

Non-residents: Boats, $10 for the first person and $4 for each additional adult; children and seniors, $1. Electric trolling motors, $17.

Season discount passes available.

GYMS

Carrboro Century Center

At the heart of downtown Carrboro, the Century Center offers classes for children in gymnastics, dance, cooking, drama, art, and more. During the fall and winter, children under six can play games with blocks and toys in the Century Hall, Tuesday mornings from 10am to 11:30am, for $3 per person. The Lollipops Series features special events for children by various performers— storytellers, puppet shows, plays, and live music—registration and a small admission fee required. The auditorium, a remnant from this building's days as a church, has high ceilings, a stage, renovated bathrooms backstage, a wooden floor, and tall windows.

Hours: Monday through Friday 9am - 5pm, and for programs.

Contact Info:
Phone: (919) 918-7385
Website: townofcarrboro.com/rp/cc.htm
Street address: 100 North Greensboro Street, Carrboro

Bathrooms: yes
Stroller-friendly: yes
Food nearby: yes
Picnic-friendly: no
Recommended ages: varies

Cost: varies

Chapel Hill Community Center

The newly renovated Community Center has a new wooden floor and improved lockers. The gymnasium has basketball goals and a climbing wall, open to the public at various times during the week and weekend, and for registered youth basketball league or after-school play. During weekday mornings, parents and toddlers can gather to play in the gym with toys provided or with your own. Check the Community Center for dates and times. Register for classes through the Chapel Hill Parks and Recreation Department.

Hours: gymnasium hours vary with specific programs throughout the week.

Contact Info:
Phone: (919) 968-2790 Center; (919) 968-2784 Chapel Hill Parks and Recreation Department
Website: www.chapelhillparks.org/rec_centers.php
Street address: 120 South Estes Drive, Chapel Hill

Bathrooms: yes
Stroller-friendly: yes
Food nearby: yes
Picnic-friendly: yes
Recommended ages: any

Cost: free to residents

Chapel Hill-Carrboro YMCA

The YMCA in Chapel Hill has nice facilities with child care for parents and offers youth programs in swimming, spring and fall soccer, T-ball, and basketball. The Y philosophy emphasizes team work, fun, and total participation.

A variety of summer camps for rising kindergartners through high school feature sports, crafts, songs, games, and outdoor activities at Camp Clearwater, just south of town. Other camps focus on cooking, art, acting and movie-making, cooking, or science and outdoor education. The popular after-school program provides age-assembled groups a snack and time for homework as well as play.

The Y-Princesses and Y-Guides programs offer fathers the opportunity to play games, earn feathers, and spend time with their son or daughter. They camp, hold cookouts, and march in the Christmas Parade. Older children, fourth grade through high school, can participate in the similar program of Trailblazers and Trailmates. Both programs are open to the public, though members receive a discount on registration.

The pool is open for free swim only to members, but swimming lessons here are very highly regarded and registration can be competitive. Get in line early for a spot in the swimming classes.

Hours: varies with programs

Contact Info:
Phone: (919) 442-9622
Website: www.chcymca.org
Street address: 980 Martin Luther King Jr. Boulevard, Chapel Hill

Bathrooms: yes
Stroller-friendly: yes
Food nearby:
Picnic-friendly:
Recommended ages: any

Cost: varies, members receive discount

Chatham County YMCA

As a relatively new facility, the Chatham County YMCA continues to adapt its programming to the community's needs and interests. Membership in Pittsboro's YMCA includes access to the activities and facilities, including swimming pool, of the Chapel Hill-Carrboro YMCA. Programs include youth sports and child-parent programs, and child care is provided for children under five while parents exercise in the workout room.

Hours: Monday through Friday 6am - 8pm, Saturday 8am - 5pm, Sunday 1pm - 5pm

Contact Info:
Phone: (919) 545-YMCA (9622)
Website: www.chcymca.org/membership/chatham.php
Street address: 964 East Street, Pittsboro

Bathrooms: yes
Stroller-friendly: yes
Food nearby: yes
Picnic-friendly: no
Recommended ages: any

Cost: varies with program; membership available

Orange Tennis Club

The Orange Tennis Club offers tennis lessons for preschoolers through teenagers and adults. Classes meet at various sites including the Hillsborough high schools. Plans are underway to build a free-standing building with indoor clay courts and outdoor hard and clay courts, outdoor swimming pool, fitness center and yoga studio, and child care.

Hours: varies by class

Contact Info:
Phone: (919) 357-3467
Website: www.orangetennisclub.com
Street address: varies

Bathrooms: yes
Stroller-friendly: yes
Food nearby: no
Picnic-friendly: no
Recommended ages: pre-K and up

Cost: $75 for six classes, $120 for ten classes

Triangle Sportsplex (see also Swimming)

The fitness center at the Sportsplex has cardio and weight-training equipment for adults and a kids' gymnastics and tumbling room with classes. Nursery care is available for parents while they work out.

Of course, you can also get a workout while skating on the ice-rink. Hockey leagues for all ages play here, but during free skate times anyone can take a spin around the rink. When you're ready for a break, hot chocolate is available at the Sportsplex Grill.

Hours: varies by class

Contact Info:
Phone: (919) 644-0339
Website: www.trianglesportsplex.com
Street address: 1 Dan Kidd Drive, Hillsborough

Bathrooms: yes
Stroller-friendly: yes
Food nearby: yes
Picnic-friendly: no
Recommended ages: any

Cost: $7 walk-in, 20-punch pass $60 for members, $70 for non-members

Part 4: Road Trips!

Trips to the East

Duke Homestead

The history of Durham is, in part, the history of tobacco, and this national landmark, with its homestead, outbuildings, and early tobacco factories, constitutes a museum of early tobacco farming. In the visitors' center, the Tobacco Museum has farming tools, cigarette machinery, a shop display, and other artifacts connected to the growth, curing, and processing of tobacco. The house, built in 1852, has heart-pine walls and furnishings appropriate to the time period. In the outbuildings, tour guides explain farming and curing methods.

Special events and programs occur throughout the year, including demonstrations, archaeology activities, the Herb, Garden and Craft Festival in June, the Tobacco and Hornworm Festival in September, and Preparing the Homestead in October. The holiday tours in December include hot cider and singing.

Hours: Tuesday through Saturday 9am - 5pm

Contact Info:
Phone: (919) 477-5498
Website: www.ah.dcr.state.nc.us/Sections/hs/duke/duke.htm, www.ibiblio.org/dukehome
Street address: 2828 Duke Homestead Road, Durham

Bathrooms: yes
Stroller-friendly: yes
Food nearby: yes
Picnic-friendly: yes
Recommended ages: any

Cost: free, except for some special events

Duke Lemur Center

Established at Duke University in 1966 and located within Duke Forest, the Duke Lemur Center studies and cares for about 250 prosimian primates including 15 species of lemurs, Asian lorises, and African bushbabies. It also seeks to educate people here, and in Madagascar, about the importance of preserving this very endangered species, and offers tours of the lemur center by appointment year round.

After a brief video, well-informed guides lead small groups outside around the cages of a selection of both diurnal and nocturnal lemurs. In cool weather, the cages are covered to keep these Madagascar natives warm. In practical terms, this means the group must huddle around zippered openings roughly 5 feet wide and peer into the dimly lighted interiors. Because lemurs communicate by scent, the odor trapped inside can dampen enthusiasm, especially of younger children. However, fewer people tour in the cooler months, so viewing is easier than in the more crowded spring and summer.

The gift shop has a good selection of interesting items—stuffed lemur toys, clothing, books, even lemur tail and ear costumes—and all profits support the care of these beautiful animals. Visitors may also buy snacks and beverages, but there are no picnic tables or grassy lawns. The Lemur Center is first and foremost a scientific facility.

Call at least two weeks in advance for an appointment, especially during the more popular warm months. The helpful staff readily offers reduced fees for groups. The center allows visitors of all ages, but children younger than four may not have the attention span or understanding to appreciate looking for the lemurs in their cages.

Hours: Monday through Friday 8:30am - 4:30pm by appointment only

Contact Info:
Phone: (919) 489-3364
Website: lemur.duke.edu
Street Address: 3705 Erwin Road, Durham

Bathrooms: yes
Stroller-friendly: yes
Food nearby: no—but the gift shop does sell chips and beverages
Picnic-friendly: no
Recommended ages: 4 and up

Cost: adults $7, children (3-12) $4, toddlers (1-2) $1, senior citizens $4, college students $5

Durham Bulls

Taking in a Bulls game is a classic Triangle pasttime and a lot of fun for families. Wool E. Bull races a child around the bases (and loses), Lucky the Wonder Dog performs tricks, and, if the children get antsy, the updated playground near right field has a play structure with slides and inflatable games. The food on the concourse ranges from typical to delicious, especially the barbecue and freshly squeezed lemonade.

Then there's the baseball. The Durham Bulls are a AAA minor league farm team for the Tampa Bay Rays, which means a chance to see future major league players. The Durham Bulls Athletic Park is a great place to watch a game, as any seat has a good view, and the fans are enthusiastic and loyal. This team was the subject of the movie "Bull Durham," and the famous "Hit Bull Win Steak/ Hit Grass Win Salad" sign remains from the original home of the Bulls, the Durham Athletic Park.

Across the street, the American Tobacco Warehouse Historic District has several family-friendly restaurants as well as waterfalls, sidewalks, a large grassy area, a water tower from the old days, and a huge whistle that still sounds on weekdays at 7am, lunch break, and quittin' time.

Hours: afternoon and evening games, April through September

Contact Info:
Phone: (919) 687-6500, (919) 956-BULL Ticket Line
Website: www.durhambulls.com
Street Address: 409 Blackwell Street, Durham

Bathrooms: yes
Stroller-friendly: yes, to a point
Food nearby: yes
Picnic-friendly: yes, especially in the Diamond View grassy section
Recommended ages: all, of course!

Cost: Field Reserved, $6.50; Terrace Reserved, $6; Terrace View, $5.50; Diamond View, $4.50.The Bulls use a variable-price system, so add $2 to all ticket prices for Friday and Saturday games, except for lawn and standing-room-only tickets.

Eno River State Park

The Eno River State Park has thousands of acres of protected land and over twenty miles of maintained trails in five access points—Cole Mill and Pump Station on the eastern side, Few's Ford, Pleasant Green, and Cabe Lands in the western section—as well as the City of Durham's park, West Point on the Eno. The websites below have good maps and descriptions of trails and facilities. The Cole Mill Road and Few's Ford sections have restrooms, picnic areas, and canoe access. All of the sites have trails with some point of interest, be it dramatic bluffs, thick stands of laurel, or the remains of an old homeplace, with stately oaks, daffodils, and rock foundation. Pets on leashes are permitted, but bicycles and motorized traffic are not.

West Point on the Eno has five miles of trails and three historic buildings at the park: a house, a packhouse, and a still-functioning grist mill. The buildings are open on weekends for tours, or call to schedule a weekday tour. The Schoolhouse of Wonder hosts field trips and runs spring and summer camps. Throughout the year, various events focus on the wildlife of the river such as wafting with River Dave, wildflower hikes, and the annual Festival for the Eno.

Hours: Pump Station and Few's Ford open 8am. Cole Mill and Cabe Lands open 8:30am. Call or check website for closing times. West Point on the Eno: daily 8am - dusk. Buildings open mid-March through mid-December, Saturday and Sunday 1pm - 5pm, or by appointment.

Contact Info:
Phone: (919) 383-1686 Eno River State Park, (919) 471-1623 West Point on the Eno, (919) 477-4549 Eno River Association and Festival for the Eno
Website: www.enoriver.org, www.enoriver.org/eno/parks/ERSP/East.html, www.enoriver.org/eno/parks/ERSP/West.html, www.enoriver.org/eno/parks/WestPoint/westpoint.html

Street Address: 6101 Cole Mill Road, Durham. West Point on Eno: 5101 North Roxboro Road, Durham

Bathrooms: yes
Stroller-friendly: yes, though jog stroller or backpack would probably work best
Food nearby: yes
Picnic-friendly: yes
Recommended ages: any

Cost: free

Festival for the Eno

Every July 4th and closest weekend, people attend the Festival for the Eno to hear locally and nationally known musicians of every genre, as well as watch cloggers and dancers, see demonstrations, and support and learn about the Eno River Association's progress in preserving land along this river. Parking near the West Point on the Eno is limited, but satellite parking and buses accommodate the traffic.

Every hour brings something new to the children's stage—storytellers, magicians, musicians, and more. Children love exploring the festival, looking at the jewelry, clothing, honey and jams for sale, running through mist tents, getting their faces painted, examining turtles or other creatures brought by the Museum of Life and Science, and dipping their feet in the Eno River. Prepare to be hot, and take water, hats, bugspray, sunscreen, and comfortable shoes. Then forget all about the indoors. The cool water of the Eno River and the lushness of trees in a North Carolina summer are a solace all their own.

Hours: July 4th and closest Saturday and Sunday, 10am – 6pm

Contact Info:
Phone: (919) 471-1623 West Point on the Eno, (919) 477-4549 Eno River Association and Festival for the Eno
Website: www.enoriver.org, www.enoriver.org/eno/parks/WestPoint/westpoint.html
Street Address: 5101 North Roxboro Road, Durham

Bathrooms: yes
Stroller-friendly: yes, though jog stroller or backpack would probably work best
Food nearby: yes
Picnic-friendly: yes
Recommended ages: any

Cost: $20 adults

Ganyard Hill Farm

Ganyard Hill Farm has perhaps the best-known pumpkin patch in the area. Located in east Durham, it offers hayrides, a haystack, farmyard animals, and of course pumpkins.

It has three different mazes, of corn, sorghum, and hay bales for the younger children. There are many picnic tables and a foot-operated hand-washing station. Visitors can even pick cotton. The farm store sells canned goods and produce. Group rates and party packages are available.

Hours: end of September through Halloween

Contact Info:
Phone: (919) 596-8728
Website: www.pumpkincountry.com
Street address: 319 Sherron Road, Durham

Bathrooms: yes
Stroller-friendly: yes
Food nearby: yes
Picnic-friendly: yes
Recommended ages: any

Cost: $12.50 includes a pumpkin, children under 2 free (unless they choose a pumpkin).

North Carolina Museum of Life and Science

Located at the end of a residential street, this gem of a family-friendly museum has a lot to do and look at, in both the changing and permanent exhibits. Outside, the playground has sound instruments to play with, structures to explore, and room to run around. The farmyard features such domesticated animals as turkeys and rabbits. The wild animal habitats protect black bears, red wolves and lemurs. The butterfly house has good educational information, and the plants and benches make it a lovely quiet place to watch the beautiful butterflies. New outdoor exhibits examine wind and wetlands.

Nearby, Grayson's Café offers sandwiches, soups and salads and a children's menu. The scenic train ride through the woods lasts ten minutes, and though it costs extra, it is popular, so if you plan to ride, get there early. The train runs every half hour, from 10:30am until 4pm, weather permitting.

Inside, the main building has permanent exhibits on space exploration, weather phenomenon and study, and geology. Changing exhibits vary but usually have interactive displays and hands-on activities. Daily events, such as feeding the animals and releasing butterflies into the conservatory, teach additional lessons about science in engaging ways. The gift shop has some interesting science-related items that are unusual and educational.

The museum hosts field trips and children's programs including the well-regarded science summer camps they offer both in Durham and in Chapel Hill. Birthday party packages are also available.

Hours: January to September, Monday through Saturday 10am - 5pm, Sunday 12pm - 5pm. September through December, Tuesday through Saturday 10am - 5pm, Sunday 12pm - 5pm. Museum members admitted at 9am weekdays. Closed Thanksgiving, Christmas, and New Year's Day.

Contact Info:
Phone: (919) 220-5429
Website: www.ncmls.org
Street address: 433 Murray Road, Durham

Bathrooms: yes
Stroller-friendly: yes
Food nearby: yes
Picnic-friendly: yes
Recommended ages: any

Cost: adults $10.85, adults 65 and up $8.85, children 3-12 $7.85, children under 3 free. Military discount available and museum memberships available. Durham County residents admitted free on Wednesday afternoons 1pm - 6pm. Train rides are an additional charge of $2.00 per person. Ornithopher rides are $1.00 (tokens available in Catch the Wind).

   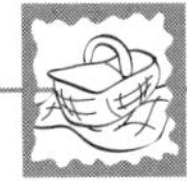

Sarah P. Duke Gardens

One of the most wonderful places on earth, Duke Gardens has both lots to do and a pretty setting for doing nothing. Children find a baffling delight in scurrying down the elegant stone stairs and slope, and running around the flower bed circle, exhilarated by this special place. When you finally drag them away from the entrance, they'll enjoy following the criss-cross paths of the Terrace Garden and examining the flowers. On springtime Saturdays, check the gazebo first to make sure there's not a wedding in progress—you don't want to startle the violinist. If the coast is clear, everyone can admire the beautiful display of flowers. The Duke Gardens are meticulously maintained, so you'll want to remind your children not to disturb the beds. The Terrace Café here serves light fare, except when it closes for the winter.

The Asiatic Arboretum has bridges, ducks to feed, artistic features, and sculpted plantings. The H. L. Blomquist Garden of Native Plants has a birdwatching gazebo in lush surroundings. At least a dozen guided tours are available for preschoolers through fifth graders, for groups or schools. Other programming includes performances, games, scavenger hunts, story times, preschool workshops and camps. Instructors are experienced and friendly. For self-guide pamphlets, call (919) 668-1708. The Doris Duke Center has a horticultural library, restrooms, and a good gift shop, and facilities are available for rent. With something new to see in every season, Duke Gardens are a rich resource for learning about plants, trees, and the long history between plants and the people who cultivate them.

Hours: daily 8am - dusk. Doris Duke Center: Monday through Saturday 9am - 6pm, Sunday 12pm - 5pm. Closed on major holidays.

Contact Info:
Phone: (919) 684-3698
Website: www.hr.duke.edu/dukegardens/index.html
Street Address: 426 Anderson Street, Durham

Bathrooms: yes
Stroller-friendly: yes
Food nearby: yes
Picnic-friendly: yes
Recommended ages: any

Cost: free, but the parking is not

The Scrap Exchange

This non-profit arts and crafts center recycles items such as Styrofoam, cardboard tubes, paper, stickers, thin silver foil, and more—materials from industry that are clean and suitable, with imagination, for turning into objects of art, science, and fun. The warehouse and workshop area are full of a huge variety of materials, and the gallery exhibits works by artists who create with recycled materials. Some artists come to teach classes on such techniques as collage and mosaics. The Scrap Exchange also has party and event packages.

Hours: Monday, Tuesday, Wednesday, and Friday 11am - 5pm, Thursday 11am - 6pm, Saturday 10am - 5pm, Sunday 12pm - 5pm

Contact Info:
Phone: (919) 688-6960
Website: www.scrapexchange.org
Street address: 548 Foster Street, Durham

Bathrooms: yes
Stroller-friendly: yes
Food nearby: yes
Picnic-friendly: no
Recommended ages: preschool and up

Cost: varies

Carolina Hurricanes

The area's only top-level professional hockey team, Raleigh's Carolina Hurricanes won the Stanley Cup in 2006, and the high quality of play continues in the fast-paced, hard-hitting action of the fastest game on ice. They put on a show for kids too, with appearances by their mascot, Stormy, and on-ice games and contests. Though on the loud side, it's definitely entertaining. The RBC Center features the typical arena fare, with some local favorites thrown in, such as Goodberry's frozen custard.

Hours: Pre-season and regular season, September through April. Box office opens at 10am on weekdays, three hours before game on weekends.

Contact Info:
Phone: (919) 861-2300 RBC Center, (919) 861-2323 event information recording, (919) 834-4000 Raleigh/Durham Ticketmaster
Website: hurricanes.nhl.com
Street address: 1400 Edwards Mill Road, Raleigh

Bathrooms: yes
Stroller-friendly: yes
Food nearby: yes
Picnic-friendly: no
Recommended ages: any

Cost: $20 and up

Marbles Kids Museum

Playspace and Exploris merged in 2006 to create Marbles Kids Museum, with a focus on creative play in four main exhibits and adorned with marble displays. Near the front half of a real city bus, you will pass a hand-sanitizer dispenser on the wall—cleaning hands will help keep your visit healthy, for it is all hands-on fun. "Around Town" is a dramatic play area with almost a dozen different themes. Inside are a boat; a fire truck with realistic gear; an ambulance and hospital; a farm, market, and restaurant; and a post office with a place to make your own "mail" to send. At the back is a large, E-shaped train table and plenty of trains to push around. Nearby stands a tree house with puppets, a stage area, and a quiet reading nook. The separate Crawl Space provides safe amusement for babies, including a soft rocking chair for comforting. If you can drag yourself from here, the "Splash" exhibit has waterproof smocks and waterplay. A craft area lies between "Splash" and the popular three-story pirate ship. Upstairs, the "2 B Me" exhibit focuses on self-expression, with singing, music, art, and very simple web design.

The museum offers birthday party packages and summer camps. The Corner Store sells snack food and educational toys such as a refrigerator marbles game and gyroscopes. Tucked around the counter, hot coffee and tea are available for the adults. The IMAX theater shows five movies. Tickets are available by phone to museum members, and online and at the desk and ticket booth for everyone else.

Hours: Tuesday through Saturday 9am - 5pm, Sunday 12pm - 5pm. Closed Monday "with some exceptions."

Contact Info:

Phone: (919) 834-4040, (919) 882-IMAX (IMAX theatre)
Website: marbleskidsmuseum.org
Street address: 201 East Hargett Street, Raleigh

Bathrooms: yes
Stroller-friendly: yes
Food nearby: yes
Picnic-friendly:
Recommended ages: any

Cost: $5 for adults and children over 1; memberships available

North Carolina Museum of Art

The Museum of Art in Raleigh has art and events the whole family can enjoy. The museum's collection is large and diverse, often supplemented with interesting and popular exhibits. The building itself is large, with lots of stairs, and children may tire well before seeing everything, so it is best to plan ahead. Start in the Collection Connection Learning Center, a room loaded with things to help children enjoy the art they see.

Or go on a Saturday, when the museum hosts workshops and craft activities for children and families, or attend, for a small fee, one of the children's performances, such as puppet shows, for children five years and older. During the summer, art-inclined children from first to twelfth grades can enroll in art camps.

The museum has a store with interesting items from books to toys. A nice restaurant downstairs, Blue Ridge, offers lunch Tuesday through Friday, and brunch on Sunday. It has excellent food, a bit on the pricey side, and is comfortable, with windows looking out over the museum's pretty and extensive grounds.

Not all the art is inside. On the museum's 164 acres are trails, sculptures, and statuary to explore without inside voices. During the summer, the museum hosts outdoor movies and music concerts, with food vendors, perfect for dancing and picnicking under the stars.

Hours: Tuesday through Thursday and Saturday 9am - 5pm, Friday 9am - 9pm, Sunday 10am - 5pm. Closed Monday. Closed July 4th, Veterans Day, Thanksgiving Day, Christmas Eve, and Christmas Day. Museum park open daily, dawn to dusk.

Contact Info:
Phone: (919) 839-6262 administrative offices, (919) 715-5923 box office, (919) 664-6838 Blue Ridge restaurant reservations
Website: www.ncartmuseum.org
Street Address: 2110 Blue Ridge Road, Raleigh

Bathrooms: yes
Stroller-friendly: yes
Food nearby: yes
Picnic-friendly: yes
Recommended ages: any, but especially preschool and up

Cost: free; some exhibits and special events have an admission fee. Discounts available for senior citizens aged 65 and over and museum members.

North Carolina Museum of Natural History

Rocks and dinosaurs in the same building are a combination hard to beat, but this museum also has a two-story diorama of the different North Carolina environments. Live animals, such as snapping and painted turtles swim in tanks next to stuffed beaver and deer in a woodland setting. A waterfall in the mountains end has schools of live fish and stuffed birds in trees.

Daily programs such as live science shows, meeting the animals, and story-readings of books about nature can make a visit special, and the changing exhibits are very popular, though they do often charge an admission fee.

When walking and looking take their toll, the museum's café has yogurt as well as the standard chips and drinks fare. The gift shop is large and has inexpensive gadgets, pencils, and stickers as well as jewelry, housewares, and art.

Hours: Monday through Saturday 9am - 5pm, Sunday 12pm - 5pm

First Fridays-- on the first Friday of every month (except as noted) the Museum stays open until 9pm. Closed New Year's Day, Thanksgiving, Christmas Eve, and Christmas Day. The Discovery Room, Naturalist Center, and Living Conservatory closed Monday.

Contact Info:
Phone: (919) 733-7450, (877) 4-NATSCI; TTY (919) 715-6464
Website: www.naturalsciences.org
Street address: 11 West Jones Street, Raleigh

Bathrooms: yes
Stroller-friendly: yes
Food nearby: yes
Picnic-friendly: yes
Recommended ages: any, but especially preschool and up

Cost: free; special exhibits may have admission fee

Pullen Park

Pullen Park is Raleigh's large, historic park, but what really matters is that it has places to play and an excellent scenic railroad. The train itself is colorful and well-maintained, and the track circles the playground and little Lake Howell, going through two tunnels, over bridges, and through a pretty garden. The playground, though ready for an update, has plenty of room to run, many swings, about half a dozen bouncy animals on springs, and slides. Tucked in the corner is a ride for little ones—boats that go in a circle. A real caboose is open for kids as well.

The Dentzel carousel's hand-carved animals have been restored several times over the years, and now a wooden building protects it from the elements. Nearby stand statues of Andy and Opie, donated by TVLand to commemorate the Andy Griffith Show. Beyond them lies Lake Howell, with scenic bridges and ducks and geese. Paddle boats are available for rent and provide an excellent way to enjoy this pretty area.

The park also includes an aquatics center, an arts center with classes and summer camps, a theatre with year-round performances, and ball fields and tennis courts. A concessions stand offers snacks and drinks. To beat the crowds, go early or late in the day. Shelters are available for gatherings and parties, but call far in advance as these book up quickly.

Hours: March to May, Monday through Friday 10am - 5:30pm, Saturday 10am - 6:30pm, Sunday 1pm - 6:30pm.

May through August, Monday through Friday 10am - 5:30pm, Saturday 10am - 7:30pm, Sunday, 1pm - 7:30pm. Memorial Day, July 4th, and Labor Day, 10am - 7:30pm.

September through October, Monday through Friday 10am - 5pm, Saturday 10am - 6:30pm, Sunday 1pm - 6:30pm.

November, Monday through Friday 10am - 4pm, Saturday 10am - 5pm, Sunday 1pm - 5pm. Closed Thanksgiving. Closed December to March.

Contact Info:

Phone: (919) 831-6468
Website: www.raleighnc.gov
Street address: 520 Ashe Avenue, Raleigh

Bathrooms: yes
Stroller-friendly: yes
Food nearby: yes
Picnic-friendly: yes
Recommended ages: any

Cost: free; tickets $1 each

Pump It Up

Pump It Up is an indoor playground of huge inflatable structures for bouncing, sliding, jumping, and climbing. It makes a great destination when the weather is too wet, cold, or hot, or for a group event or party. For a set amount of time, one room and all the structures in it are open for playing and burning off energy. The big slide is a lot of fun. There's some noise of the generators that keep the structures inflated, and music to keep the mood festive. Children four years and older may enjoy it more than the little ones, who can be hard to supervise and may find the noise and activity intimidating.

The weekday special "Pop-in Playtime" offers a one-hour drop-in session, with separate times for children under six and older children. Otherwise, you'll need a group and an advance reservation. Pump It Up offers several birthday packages with pizza, drinks, and even goodie bags. Don't forget your socks!

Hours: by reservation

Contact Info:
Phone: (919) 828-3344
Website: www.pumpitupparty.com
Street address: 10700 World Trade Boulevard Suite 112, Raleigh

Bathrooms: yes
Stroller-friendly: yes
Food nearby: yes
Picnic-friendly: no
Recommended ages: any, but especially 4 and up

Cost: varies by size of group and package; $7 per child for Pop-In Play

Umstead Park

Raleigh's five thousand acres of wooded park has eleven trails for pedestrians, mountain bikes, and horses, all designated either easy or moderate—but be sure to follow the markers. The park has two sections, Crabtree and Reedy Creek. The Crabtree section, located off highway 70 on Umstead Parkway, has a visitors center and the park office. Two easy trails lead from here, as well as the longer Sycamore Trail. The Reedy Creek section, near I-40 off Harrison Avenue, has the popular Company Mill Trail that leads to the dam at the site of the former Company Mill, a pleasant spot for a picnic. Maps of trails and facilities are available online.

Fishing, with a license, is permitted in the park's creeks and three lakes. Canoes and rowboats are available for rent, daily in the summer and on weekends in the spring and fall. Tent and trailer campgrounds have showers, grills, and picnic areas, while backpack camping sites are available by reservation. The park also has three group camping sites with facilities. Picnic areas have water and restrooms; shelters are available for rent.

Throughout the year, rangers give talks about the history or wildlife of the park. Many workshops and educational materials are available, and the Visitors' Center has interactive and photography exhibits about the park's construction and natural history. Pets are permitted in the park but must be attached to a leash and accompanied at all times by their people.

Hours: daily, November through February 8am - 6pm; March and October 8am - 7pm; April, May, September 8am - 8pm; June through August 8am - 9pm. Closed Christmas Day. Park office open daily 8am - 5pm. Closed Christmas Day. Visitor's center open November through February 8am - 5pm; March through October 9am - 6pm. Closed Christmas Day.

Contact Info:
Phone: (919) 571-4170
Website: www.stateparks.com/william_b_umstead.html www.ncparks.gov/Visit/parks/wium/main.php
Street address: 8801 Glenwood Avenue, Raleigh

Bathrooms: yes
Stroller-friendly: no
Food nearby: no
Picnic-friendly: yes
Recommended ages: any

Cost: free; boat rentals $5 for first hour, $3 for each additional hour

Trips to the West

Blueberry Hill

In addition to the farm listed here, there may be more pick-your-own farms during the season, as the number of organic farms increase in the area. Check online sites such as www.pickyourown.org or www4.ncsu.edu.

These pick-your-own blueberries are grown organically.

Hours: July to September; call for times

Contact Info:
Phone: (919) 923-3137
Street address: 8411 NC Hwy 86, Cedar Grove

Burlington City Park and Carousel

Burlington's City Park offers 75 acres of outdoor entertainment, ball fields, shaded grassy areas, picnic tables and grills, concessions, and, last but certainly not least, an amusement park. The park hosts many annual events, such as a summer music concert series and the Burlington Carousel Festival in September. Several shelters and buildings are available for rent, including packages for children's parties at the amusement park.

The amusement park has a well-run, varied assortment of rides, including boats, cars, and airplanes. The carousel, a hundred-year-old Dentzel, has beautiful animals, some with real hair tails. The Stinson Organ Company organ plays calliope versions of such songs as "Toot Toot Tootsie Goodbye," for the authentic carousel experience. The animals on the outer edge do not move up and down but are stationary, a welcome option for younger or more cautious children.

The train has a good-looking station, and the engine itself is modeled after the one first used in constructing the Continental Railroad. The track is not long, but the train makes three trips around, including going through a tunnel and over two bridges over the creek that runs through the park. Before the park closes for the winter, the park presents a Haunted Train Ride for Halloween.

The sunny playground has a large, new play structure on mulch. There are four swings and a popular sand box. Benches around the playground and throughout the amusement park provide places to rest and enjoy a snack from home or park fare from the concessions stand, such as popcorn, nachos, cotton candy, and slushies.

Hours: daily, dawn to dusk. Amusement park: summer season, Tuesday through Thursday 10am - 1pm and 5pm - 8pm; Friday 10am - 1pm and 5pm - 9pm; Saturday 11am - 9pm; Sunday 1pm - 7pm. Closed Monday. Fall season, weekends only, Saturday 11am - 9pm, Sunday 1pm - 7pm . Closed November 1 through March 20.

Contact Info:
Burlington Recreation and Parks Department
Phone: (336) 222-5030
Website: www.burlingtonnc.gov/index.asp?NID=233
Street Address: South Church Street at South Main Street, Burlington

Bathrooms: yes
Stroller-friendly: yes
Food nearby: yes
Picnic-friendly: yes
Recommended ages: any

Cost: Park entrance, free. Amusement park, 75 cents a ticket, each ride one ticket. Book of 10 for $6. Thursday Special $.50 per ride. Group (100+ people) rate: $2.25 for six ride pass.

Carolina RailHawks

With the popularity of soccer, especially youth soccer, growing everywhere, the area recently gained the United Soccer League RailHawks. The men's team ranks in the top ten and won the Southern Derby in 2007. The women's team plays throughout the spring. For the excitement of live, professional soccer, this is the place.

Hours: April through September; game times vary, though most occur on weekend evenings.

Contact Info:
Phone: (919) 859-KICK (5425) Carolina RailHawks box office
Website: carolinarailhawks.com
Street address: WakeMed Soccer Park, 201 Soccer Park Drive, Cary

Bathrooms: yes
Stroller-friendly: yes
Food nearby: yes
Picnic-friendly: no
Recommended ages: any

Cost: tickets start at $10, season ticket packages available.

Cedarock Park and Historical Farm

The 414 beautiful acres of Cedarock Park make a lovely refuge for outdoor rest and recreation, a natural destination for both celebratory family gatherings and a quiet mid-winter outing. With two disc golf courses, volleyball, basketball, and horseshoe courts, creekside, equestrian, and backpack camping, fishing, and trails, this park has a lot of options for fun.

A favorite site is the waterfall at the old dam, originally a grist mill in the early 1800s and rebuilt in 1950. Trails wind throughout the park, including six miles of bridle trail. Hiking paths are shorter, from 1.4 miles long to .2 mi; between the five of them you could create as long a hike as you like. The mountain bike trails are reportedly not terribly rugged and constitute about six miles of single track. Although swimming in the creek is not permitted, canoes are available and fishing is definitely allowed.

The playground has two structures, the larger one an exciting three floors high, with slides, a bouncing mechanism, and monkey bars with an interesting twist. The nearby park office has bathrooms, and the Visitors' Center contains a museum of the park. The historic farm near the entrance has outbuildings, antique and replica farm equipment, and animals. For two weekends in February, the Historical Farm Tours explore the history of the farm. Other special events occur during the year including the Preserving Our Heritage Festival in August, Run at the Rock in December, and birdwatching meetings. Seven picnic shelters are available for rent, in case you have a special event of your own.

Hours: daily 8am - 6pm

Contact Info:
Phone: (336) 570-6759, (336) 229-2410 shelter reservations
Website: www.alamance-nc.com/Alamance-NC/Departments/Recreation/Parks/Cedarock/
Street address: 4242 R. Dean Coleman Rd, Burlington, NC

Bathrooms: yes
Stroller-friendly: yes
Food nearby: no
Picnic-friendly: yes
Recommended ages: any

Cost: free

Greensboro Children's Museum

The Greensboro Children's Museum has twenty interactive and hands-on exhibits. In the dramatic play exhibit "Our Town," children can go to the market with a real cash register, pretend to dine in the colorful café, perform on stage, and work at a bank. Creation Station has all kinds of materials, from watercolors to recycled items, for children to turn into art. While older children explore and play, toddlers and babies can investigate the soft and stimulating Tot Lot. The Construction Zone explores the way houses are built, and Nonie's House reconstructs the way houses used to look, so that children can compare how they live now with the 1930's. There's much more to do here—a climbing wall, bubbles fun, train sets, airplanes, race cars, sand and water play, and an outdoor area with a garden, so bring plenty of energy and perhaps a few snacks.

Events such as puppet shows, skits, story times, camps, and special speakers change monthly, so check the website's calendar or call the museum. A teacher's guide, available online, contains lesson plans to connect the museum's exhibits with the North Carolina education curriculum. The gift shop has the variety of educational items of Toys and Co. toy store, and Georgie's Café provides a place to eat—but call ahead if you plan to eat there, as the café is sometimes reserved. Museum party packages are available.

Hours: Monday 9am - noon (members only), Tuesday 9am - 7pm, Wednesday, Thursday, Saturday 9am - 5pm, Friday 9am - 8pm, Sunday 1pm - 5pm. Closed July 4, Thanksgiving Day, Christmas Eve, Christmas Day, New Year's Eve, New Year's Day, and Easter Sunday.

Contact Info:
Phone: (336) 574-2898
Website: www.gcmuseum.com
Street address: 220 N. Church Street, Greensboro

Bathrooms: yes
Stroller-friendly: yes
Food nearby: yes
Picnic-friendly: yes
Recommended ages: 0 to 10 years old

Cost: Adults and children over 1 year $6, senior citizens $5. Friday after 5pm and Sunday $3. Children under 1 year-old, free.

Maple View Farm and Country Store

One of the real treats of life is to sit in a rocker on the Maple View Country Store porch, enjoying a scoop of Maple View Farm ice cream and watching the hard-working cows graze on the farm in the distance. Even if you could never tire of their fabulous vanilla ice cream, they feature special sundaes, unique flavors such as Carolina Crunch, and unusual treats such as pineapple basil sorbet. This is the place to bring out-of-town guests.

If the rockers are full, or the porch too confining for rambling little ones, the grassy area has picnic tables, a place to hitch horses (not for climbing, though it is sorely tempting), and almost always a big pile of hay for playing and jumping.

The store sells other dairy products, such as milk, cream, and, in season, eggnog, as well as grass-fed beef and products and crafts from local producers. Ice cream cakes, ordered in advance, can be made with your choice of flavors and between-layer filling. Outside, vendors of fresh shrimp or other wares occasionally set up a booth near the parking lot.

Due to the international outbreak of foot and mouth disease, the farm is no longer open to the public, but the virtual tour on their website has photographs and detailed commentary. Maple View Farm has two smaller stores, one in Hillsborough near the intersection of I-85 and Hwy 86, the other in downtown Carrboro across from Weaver Street Market, which closes for a few months in the winter.

Hours: daily 12pm - 8pm

Phone: (919) 960-5535 Country Store, (919) 644-2222 Maple View Farm Ice Cream II Hillsborough, (919) 967-6842 Carrboro Store
Website: www.mapleviewfarm.com
Street Address: Country Store: 6900 Rocky Ridge Road, Hillsborough; Maple View Farm Ice Cream II: 525A Hampton Pointe Boulevard, Hillsborough; Maple View Farm Carrboro Store: 100 East Weaver Street, Carrboro

Bathrooms: yes
Stroller-friendly: yes
Food nearby: yes
Picnic-friendly: yes
Recommended ages: any

Cost: small (kids') scoop $1.25, regular scoop $2.30, two scoops $3.50. Pints and half gallons also available.

Natural Science Center of Greensboro

The Natural Science Center in Greensboro has exhibits on the sun, moon, and stars, and it especially features animals, from lemurs to poison dart frogs, from the aquarium and herpetarium to a petting zoo. Children can also see rocks that glow in the dark, make rubbings of dinosaurs, explore the water play area, and examine the fascinating exhibit on the human body. The museum's gift shop has unusual and educational toys. Programs, classes, and party packages are available.

This museum has enough to do, especially if the weather is nice and you can take advantage of the animals outside, that it is worth the drive to Greensboro. Here, with all the informative displays as well as interesting manipulatives and activities, children really can play and learn at the same time.

Hours: Monday through Saturday 9am - 5pm, Sunday 12:30pm - 5pm. Closed Thanksgiving, Christmas Day, and New Year's Day. Closes at 2pm Christmas Eve and New Year's Eve.

Animal Discovery Hours: Monday through Saturday 10am - 4pm, Sunday 12:30pm - 4pm.

Contact Info:
Phone: (336) 288-3769
Website: www.natsci.org
Street Address: 4301 Lawndale Drive, Greensboro

Bathrooms:
Stroller-friendly:
Food nearby: yes
Picnic-friendly: yes
Recommended ages: any

Cost: Adults $8, children 3-13 and seniors 65 and up $7, children under 2 free. Discount for Greensboro residents. Fee may be greater for special events and exhibitions.

North Carolina Zoo

The NC Zoo was constructed in the 1970s with the then unusual idea of protecting and exhibiting animals in surroundings resembling their native habitats. For the animals, this approach offers freedom from isolated cages. For people, it gives stirring sights such as an antelope herd sweeping down the hillside in golden afternoon light. In practical terms, it means the zoo is big and seemingly all uphill. You can enter at either the North America or Africa exhibit, but walking from one to the other covers a lot of ground. Wear comfortable clothes and shoes, and bring water and a carrier or stroller for the little ones. Strollers and wheelchairs are also available for rent. The trams, though frequent and fun to ride, can take up valuable time, so unless you have all day, you might want to focus on one continent. Africa, older and more complete, has a lot of big exhibits, with animals somewhat far away. North America's exhibits tend to be more compact and include extras for children such as a 3D ride and a Kid Zone with hands-on activities, March through October. Occasionally exhibits close temporarily, due to construction or weather, so if you hope to see a favorite animal, it's worth calling ahead or checking the website.

When kids need a break from walking and looking, Junction Plaza's endangered species carousel costs $2 a ride, March through October. Special events occur monthly, many with activities for children. The museum shops are big and, while a bit heavy on touristy souvenirs, have some educational items. The three cafés serve amusement park fare, or get your hands stamped and picnic outside the Africa entrance gates. Nearby Asheboro has fast food, and, if you're up for the search, some pretty good barbecue restaurants.

Hours: daily, April through October 9am - 5pm (use either North American or African entrance), November through March 9am - 4pm (use only North American entrance). Closed Christmas Day and in severe weather.

Contact Info:

Phone: (800) 488-0444 information line
Website: www.nczoo.org
Street address: 4401 Zoo Parkway, Asheboro

Bathrooms: yes
Stroller-friendly: yes
Food nearby: yes
Picnic-friendly: yes, outside the zoo gates; shelters available for rent
Recommended ages: any

Cost: March through November: $10 adults, $8 college students and adults 62 and older, $6 children 2-12. December, January and February, $2 off admission. Group rates available with advance registration. Memberships available.

Old Salem

Moravians founded Salem in the eighteenth century, and today Old Salem's carefully restored houses and shops comprise a museum of a way of life re-created daily by skilled interpreters such as blacksmiths, gunsmiths, shoemakers, and family members of a home. Re-enactors spin, weave, dye fabric, or practice crafts such as ribbon embroidery, and will answer questions or even teach their craft. In the bakery you can watch them make the thin wafer cookies that Moravians are known for. Fortunately, all baked goods are for sale, for they are delicious.

The Children's Museum has interactive play for children ages four through nine, with marble runs, simple weaving games, things to climb on and through, and authentic period dress up clothes. In the same building, the Toy Museum has dense displays of an interesting variety of ancient and antique toys, all in a manageable space. The small gift shop upstairs has some interesting items, and the Visitors' Center has several shops, selling toy fifes and souvenirs, as well as pricey home decorative items. Its large, well-done displays of the Moravians' history offer a good place to start your tour.

You can mail your postcards straightaway in the post office and see the historic organ in the auditorium. The Museum of Early Southern Decorative Arts exhibits furnishings and art of the southern United States from the late 1600s through the 1800s. The four historic gardens have been restored and planted with historical accuracy, so viewing these outdoor

Hours: January and February, Tuesday through Saturday 9am - 5:30pm, Sunday 12:30pm - 5:30pm. March through December, Monday through Saturday 9am - 5:30pm, Sunday 12:30pm - 5:30pm. Closed Easter Sunday, Thanksgiving, Christmas Eve, and Christmas Day.

Contact Info:
Phone: (336) 721-7300 or (888) 653-7253
Website: www.oldsalem.org
Street address: 900 Old Salem Road, Winston-Salem

Bathrooms: yes
Stroller-friendly: yes
Food nearby: yes
Picnic-friendly: yes
Recommended ages: any, though school-aged children may enjoy it more

spaces is both restful and educational.

The museum hosts various events throughout the year, including puppet shows, seminars, craft workshops, and summer music shows. Summer camps allow rising first through third graders to participate in colonial activities and crafts. The Moravian Church hosts special events such as the Candle Tea, with Moravian Lovefeast coffee, at Christmas, and the stirring Easter sunrise service in the spring. During the summer, the church's sanctuary is open to visitors. Seeing Old Salem involves a lot of walking, and there is no air conditioning. Prepare accordingly and dress for the weather, so you can explore and enjoy this historic village.

Cost: All-in-One Ticket (includes all museums and garden and a self-guided tour of the Town of Old Salem, for one day or two): One Day, adults $21, children ages 6-16 $10. Two Day, adults $24, children 6-16, $10.

Two-Stop Ticket (for any two buildings of your choice) adults $14, children 6-16, $7.

Children's Museum/ Toy Museum Ticket: $6 per person.

Discounts for members of AAA, AARP, AAM and museum professionals available.

Purchase tickets at the Visitor's Center.

Shangri-la Stone Village

Up highway 86 toward Yanceyville, there stands a little stone house with a tiny stone village next to it. This is Shangri-La, the creation of the late tobacco farmer Henry Warren. At the center of the village is a mill and water tower, and a theater with performers inside. All the buildings are made of white quartz, bricks, and decorative aqua telephone line insulators. The attention to detail makes these structures completely charming.

This category of art has been called "outsider art," a way to draw folks in for company, so feel free to wander around the village and examine the structures. The words out front say it all: "Shangri-la. Let me live in a house by the side of the road and be a friend to man.- H.L.W. 1972."

Hours: dawn to dusk

Contact Info:
Street address: Hwy 86, Prospect Hill

Bathrooms: no
Stroller-friendly: no
Food nearby: no
Picnic-friendly: no
Recommended ages: any

Cost: free

Snow Camp Outdoor Drama

The drama tradition of Snow Camp arose from the community's desire to preserve the area's Quaker history. The two main performances, "Sword of Peace" and "Pathway to Freedom," depict the Quakers' struggle to adhere to their pacifism and other religious beliefs in the face of oppression and violence. The actors, drawn from the community, nearby Greensboro, and area colleges, give memorable and moving performances and beautiful singing.

In addition to these two plays, the Snow Camp Drama Society puts on a children's show and a Broadway musical, two festivals, and a summer drama camp. The outdoor theater sits in a cluster of historic buildings, so be sure to check out the exhibits nearby. Enjoy the scenic drive to Snow Camp, bring plenty of bug spray, and prepare to experience a local tradition in outdoor drama.

Hours: end of June through August, Thursday, Friday, and Saturday 8pm. Children's show, Saturday 10am.

Contact Info:
Phone: (336) 376-6948 or (800) 726-5115
Website: www.snowcampdrama.com
Street address: 1 Drama Road, Snow Camp

Bathrooms: yes
Stroller-friendly: yes
Food nearby: yes
Picnic-friendly: no
Recommended ages: any

Cost: $14 for adults, $6 for children under 11, $12 for adults 60 and up. Children's show on Saturday mornings, $5. Season tickets $40. Group of 15 or more, $12 adults, $5 children.

TRIPS TO THE SOUTH

American Tobacco Trail

This trail, built on the former Durham Railroad bed, provides miles of greenway for walking, riding bikes, jogging, or, in some places, horseriding. When connections and pedestrian bridges are completed, the trail eventually will lead south from downtown Durham all the way to New Hill. Currently there are three main segments: a paved trail north of Interstate 40, a three-mile trail just south of the interstate, and the final, longer section to New Hill. At some trail heads, there are bathrooms and parking. At either end of the northern paved portion, you'll find parking and maps.

The wide, paved trail starts near the Durham Bulls Athletic Park and American Tobacco Historic District, and leads south to Southpoint Crossing shopping center at the intersection of Fayetteville Road and Highway 54. This greenway, open to pedestrian and bicycle traffic, runs for more than six and half miles through woods and behind neighborhoods. Along the trail, there are restaurants or places to stop, such as at mile 3 and mile 5, and of course at either of the segment's ends. Intermittent benches provide places to rest and watch rollerbladers go by. A pedestrian bridge over I-40 is planned.

Across the interstate, a largely unpaved, but smooth, wide trail leads three miles, from Massey Chapel Road near Southpoint Mall, to the as-yet unpassable Northeast Creek Trestle. The best access to this part is from the Scott King Road intersection. Nearly half a mile of paved trail from Renaissance Parkway to Massey Chapel will open when construction in this area finishes.

Hours: dawn to dusk

Contact Info:
Website: www.triangletrails.org/ATT.HTM
Street address: Intersection of Morehead Avenue and Blackwell Street; Southpoint Crossing, Highway 54 at Fayetteville Street, Durham.

Bathrooms: at available restaurants or businesses only, on northern portion; some bathrooms along southern end.
Stroller-friendly: yes
Food nearby: at various intersections
Picnic-friendly: no
Recommended ages: any

Cost: free

From the other side of the trestle, another roughly six miles of trail ends at New Hope Church Road. This part is open to equestrians as well as pedestrians and bicyclists. In this southern-most part of Durham County into Wake County, the trail crosses state gamelands, so users of the trail are advised to wear bright orange or go on Sundays, when hunting is not allowed. A helpful users guide at the website is very informative and easy to use.

The House in the Horseshoe

*6 "The House in the Horseshoe" may sound like an innovation of the ship-in-a-bottle, but in fact it's the first major dwelling on the "uplands" of North Carolina, built overlooking a bend (horseshoe) in the Deep River near Sanford, just across the line into Moore County. The house, built around 1770, still has bullet holes from the War-- the Revolutionary War. Later inhabited by four-term governor Benjamin Williams, the house now contains colonial and Revolutionary-War era furnishings.

The best time to go might be on one of the three event days, especially the battle reenactment held the first weekend in August. Musket demonstrations and other hands-on activities are available to scheduled groups upon request. The Visitors' Center has an exhibit and sells a few souvenirs of the house.

While you're in the neighborhood, Sanford, to the east, has well-known Cole Pottery. To the southeast, Cameron has nurseries and antiques. Ramble even farther south and visit the Sandhills Community College Horticultural Gardens, with seven different gardens over twenty-seven acres.

Hours: Tuesday through Saturday 9am - 5pm. Closed Sunday, Monday, and major holidays.

Contact Info:
Phone: (910) 947-2051
Website: www.ah.dcr.state.nc.us/Sections/HS/horsesho/horsesho.htm
Street Address: 288 Alston House Road, Sanford

Bathrooms: yes
Stroller-friendly: no
Food nearby: no
Picnic-friendly: yes
Recommended ages: 5 and up

Cost: free; donations accepted

Along county highways, signs for pick-your-own and pre-picked strawberries will pop up like spring flowers in front of farms. Below is listed a well-known site, but many more feature good, even organic berries. The map of the Piedmont Farm Tour, freely available around town near the end of April, provides information on local farms, even if you don't take the tour. Since this is also the prime time for strawberries, you may find an appealing farm close to you. Also check sites such as www.pickyourown.org/NCpiedmont.htm.

Jean's Berry Patch

Bring your own containers and spend an early spring morning picking your own strawberries! Be sure to call first, as this farm is a popular spot, especially on Saturdays.

Children are welcome, but, of course, not pets.

Hours: April through June 5, Monday through Friday 7:30am - 7:30pm, Saturday 7:30am - 4pm or until picked over. After 12 noon, call about availability.

Contact Info:
Phone: (919) 362-5800
Website: www.jeansberrypatch.com
Street address: 3003 N. NC Hwy 751, Apex

Bathrooms: yes
Stroller-friendly: no
Food nearby: strawberries, at least
Picnic-friendly: yes
Recommended ages: any

Cost: varies

New Hope Valley Railway Train Rides

The New Hope Valley Railway dates back to the early 1900s, and though much of the original track, which led possibly as far as Carrboro, was moved to accommodate the building of Jordan Lake in 1974, it is still possible to ride along the same railway corridor. The Bonsal train ride and museum are pretty cool, for train lovers and normal people alike.

The roughly hour-long train ride takes you from Bonsal through countryside to New Hill and back. The ride is bumpy, of course, and loud, so while riders of any age are welcome, younger or sensitive children may not enjoy it as much as others. Morning rides sell out quickly, so plan to arrive at least an hour in advance of the departure time. Having a ticket does not guarantee a seat on the train, so board promptly. Once the train is full, it will leave, even if earlier than scheduled. It is also a good idea to call ahead to make sure the train will run the day you plan to visit, or if special arrangements are needed.

Back at the station, the museum and gift shop have old photographs and equipment, postcards, snacks, and train memorabilia. On holidays, the museum hosts live music and special events. Outside, visitors can view old engines and the Garden Railroad, a large outdoor train set. The New Hope Valley Railway is a great attraction for children and adults fascinated by trains, and makes for an interesting family outing.

Hours: May through December, Sunday 11am, 12:15pm, 1:30pm, 2:45pm, and 4pm.

Contact Info:
Phone: (919) 362-5416
Email: info@nhvry.org
Website: www.nhvry.org
Street Address: 10 New Hill - Bonsal Road, New Hill

Bathrooms: yes
Stroller-friendly: no
Food nearby: yes
Picnic-friendly: yes
Recommended ages: any

Cost: $9 for adults, $6 for children ages 2 to 12

San-Lee Park

Though hard to find, this park has something for everyone, with woods, two lakes, trails, campgrounds, playgrounds, and children's programs.

About four miles of walking and hiking trails wander through mixed hardwoods forest and around two lakes. The mountain bike trail has challenging hills, stream crossings, sharp curves, and plenty of roots and rocks. In the midst of the woods, the stocked lakes are great for boat rides, and paddle boats and canoes are available for rent during summer weekends. Fishing is permitted from bridges or the banks, and kids can check out a set of fishing equipment for the day for free. All NC Wildlife and Resource Commission regulations apply here, so if you need a license, or any bait or tackle, visit a sporting goods store before you come.

The nature center, though a bit odorous in warm weather, has many interesting birds and snakes, and offers affordable nature programs and summer camps for children. Camping by RV, tent, or backpack is available, though you must register first. A large picnic shelter, multi-purpose room, an outdoor amphitheater, and even a large meadow, with a creek and bridge, may be reserved for events or gatherings.

Hours: daily, November through March 8am - 5pm, April and September 6:30am - 7pm, May through August 6:30am - 8pm, October 6:30am - 6pm. Closed New Year's Day, Thanksgiving (Thursday and Friday), and Christmas (December 24-26).

Contact Info:

Phone: (919) 776-6221 park office, (919) 775-2107 Lee County Parks and Recreation
Website: leecountync.gov/departments/parks-and-recreation/sanleepark/
Street address: 572 Pumping Station Road, Sanford

Bathrooms: yes
Stroller-friendly: yes
Food nearby: no
Picnic-friendly: yes
Recommended ages: any

Cost: free; paddle boats $3 per half-hour

Appendix A: Places Closed Weekly

Closed Sunday

Carolina Basketball Museum (except game days)
Chatham Community Library
Duke Homestead
Duke Lemur Center
House in the Horseshoe
Pittsboro Memorial Library
The Rocks Gemstone Mining and Trading Post

Closed Monday

Ackland Museum
Burlington City Park
Burwell School (except by appointment)
Cane Creek Reservoir
Chapel Hill Museum
Duke Homestead
Greensboro Children's Museum (except for members)
House in the Horseshoe
Jordan Lake Ranger Talks
Kidzu Children's Museum
Marbles Kids' Museum
Morehead Planetarium and Science Center
Museum of Life and Science, September through December only
North Carolina Museum of Art
Old Salem, January and February only
Talking Trees Trail at Jordan Lake Educational State Forest
The Rocks Gemstone Mining and Trading Post (except by appointment)

Closed Tuesday

Ackland Art Museum
Burwell School (except by appointment)
Cane Creek Reservoir
Chapel Hill Museum
Lake Michael
University Lake

Closed Wednesday

Cane Creek Reservoir
Lake Michael
University Lake

Closed Thursday

University Lake

Closed Friday

Carrboro Branch Library

Closed Saturday

Carolina Basketball Museum (except game days)
Duke Lemur Center

Appendix B: Good Choices in Bad Weather (Too Hot, Too Cold, or Too Wet)

Ackland Art Museum
Carolina Basketball Museum
Carrboro Branch Library
Chapel Hill Library
Chatham Community Library
Greensboro Children's Museum
Kidzu Children's Museum
Marbles Kids' Museum
Morehead Planetarium and Science Center
Natural Science Center of Greensboro
North Carolina Museum of Art
North Carolina Museum of Life and Science (although outside area is great fun)
North Carolina Natural History Museum
Orange County Public Library
Pittsboro Memorial Library
Pump It Up
The Scrap Exchange
Triangle Sportsplex

Appendix C: Festivals and Events by Month

January
Twelve Days of Christmas at the Carolina Inn

February
Burwell School opens for tours
Cedarock, Historical Farm Tours
Celebrity Dairy's Open Barn
Revolutionary War Living History Day

March
Burlington City Park amusement park opens
Cane Creek Reservoir, Lake Michael, and University Lake open—go fish!

April
Carrboro Farmers' Market opens on Wednesdays
CFSA Piedmont Farm Tour
Cool Jazz Festival
Durham Bulls—baseball season begins
Fridays on the Front Porch at the Carolina Inn begin
Jean's Berry Patch—strawberry season begins
Last Fridays begin
Shakori Hills GrassRoots Festival

May
A.D. Clark Pool opens
Bynum Front Porch Series begins
Carrboro Day
Carrboro Farmers' Market opens on Thursdays
Greek Festival
Haw River Festival
New Hope Valley Railway opens
Saxapahaw Farmers' Market opens
Shakori Hills Summer Outdoor Music Series begins

June
Hillsborough Hog Day
Meadowmont Swim Club opens
Occaneechi-Saponi Spring Festival and Powwow
Snow Camp Outdoor Drama

July
Blueberry Hill—blueberry season begins
Family Fun Day
Festival for the Eno
Fourth of July Celebrations

August
Old-Fashioned Farmer's Day

September
Carolina Hurricanes—hockey pre-season begins
Carrboro Music Festival
Celebration of the Automobile
Chatham County Fair
Felicity Day
Fiesta de la Familia
Woof-a-Palooza

October
Festifall
Ganyard Farm
Pittsboro Street Fair
Pumpkin Run
Shakori Hills GrassRoots Festival

November
Celebrity Dairy's Open Barn

December
Twelve Days of Christmas at the Carolina Inn

Appendix D: Activity by Location

Chapel Hill and Carrboro

A. D. Clark Pool
Ackland Art Museum
Adams Tract
Anderson Community Park
ArtsCenter
Bolin Creek trail
Cane Creek Reservoir
Carolina Basketball Museum
Carrboro Branch Library
Carrboro Century Center
Carrboro Day
Carrboro Elementary School Park
Carrboro Farmer's Market
Carrboro Music Festival
Cedar Falls Park
CFSA Piedmont Farm Tour
Chapel Hill Community Center
Chapel Hill Museum
Chapel Hill Public Library
Chapel Hill YMCA
Community Pool
Duke Forest
Ephesus Park
Festifall
Fiesta de la Familia
Fourth of July Celebrations
Fridays on the the Porch
Greek Festival
Hargraves Community Center and Park
Homestead Aquatic Center
Homestead Park
Kidzu Children's Museum
Lincoln Arts Center
Martin Luther King Jr. Park
Meadowmont Park
Meadowmont Swim Club
Morehead Planetarium
Neighborhood Parks
North Carolina Botanical Garden
North Carolina Collection Gallery
Paperhand Puppet Intervention
Phillips Park
Pumpkin Run
Spence's Farm
Town Commons Park
Twelve Days of Christmas at the Carolina Inn
Umstead Park
UNC Campus
University Lake
Weaver Street Market
Wilson Park

Hillsborough Area

Burwell School
Celebration of the Automobile
CFSA Piedmont Farm Tour
Cool Jazz Festival
Duke Forest
Efland Cheeks Park
Exchange Club Park
Fairview Park
Family Fun Day
Felicity Day
Hillsborough Hog Day
Historic Hillsborough Thematic Children's Tours
Lake Michael Park
Last Fridays
Little River Park
Occaneechi Mountain Park
Occaneechi-Saponi Spring Festival and Powwow
Orange County Public Library
Orange Tennis
Poet's Walk at Ayr Mount
Revolutionary War Weekend
Triangle Sportsplex
Weaver Street Market

Pittsboro Area

Bynum Front Porch Series
Carnivore Preservation Trust
Celebrity Dairy
CFSA Piedmont Farm Tour
Chatham Community Library
Chatham County Fair
Chatham County YMCA
Chatham Marketplace
Fearrington Striped Cows and Fainting Goats
Fearrington Village
First Sundays
Haw River Festival
Jordan Lake
Jordan Lake Ranger Talks
Old Fashioned Farmer's Day
Pittsboro Memorial Library
Pittsboro Street Fair
Playgrounds at Jordan Lake
Shakori Hills GrassRoots Festivals
Shakori Hills summer outdoor music series
Talking Trees Trail at Jordan Lake Educational State Forest
The Rocks Gemstone Mining and Trading Post
Town Lake Park
White Pines Nature Preserve
Woof-a-Palooza Dog Walk

INDEX